HELL'S SHADOW IN HEAVEN

By
Kal Burgess

ISBN: 979-8-9910372-2-8 (Paperback)
ISBN: 979-8-9910372-3-5 (Hardcover)

DEDICATION

This book is dedicated to Leo & Mary Pressey; John Burgess; Jaymee, Des, Everley, Eden & Lennon Kitchenham; Joshua, Rachel, Jaylynn & Brooklynn Kitchenham; Kayla, Joshua, Katie, & Lukas Ashe; Paula McCann: Krychelle, Tyler, Jayson & Leland Campbell; William, Amy, Mekhi, Mya, Brittany, Braden, & Asher Burgess. Sherry Spring. Tree. Lori McKenzie, Kathy, Bev & Sophie Gurski. And to Becky, James, Frank, Jessie wherever you are. Not to mention Keaunna. And to all the generations before and after.

ACKNOWEDGEMENTS

Thank you to my husband, John Burgess, who has made it possible to dare to dream. Without his love and support I would not have ventured into completing my book. He promised from the onset of our relationship to get me past all potholes on our road of love and life. My friends, Kathy Hagman, Sherry Spring and Lori McKenzie have encouraged me to take the leap and fulfill an item on my bucket list. Without the encouragement of my family, I know I would not have been brave enough to put my words onto paper for others to read. To the universe, I have arrived.

FOREWORD

I am writing this and sitting here watching TV. I had every one of my poems, songs, my gramp's writings and some family all finally done, yes and, my laptop crashed. Ah, life is funny. So here I am starting from nothing yet again. Originally, I typed them out on a typewriter and yes, I still have it in my closet. I love the feel of the keys and it takes me right back to typing with Miss Thompson at East Elgin Secondary School in Aylmer, ON. Whoa, that is 1974 and over 40 years ago. I was in high school then and marveling at the new electric typewriters we were going to get into class. I was taught the manual type. Sorry, off-topic. That happens folks. And thank God, I had given my sister a copy of both Gramps and my writings. Whew, that was impressive! I also have more reasons to start writing again. Backup, save, create a disc, save onto an external drive or onto a key, but do not lose your creative pieces.

I have suffered the ultimate price to protect others, and I would do it all over again. Just needed to say that aloud to the universe. I do not care what obstacles and doubts I come up against, I will continue to be ME. As reassurance I had my cards read and it was told to me that I have paid the price for many and they are appreciative for that, whether they have voiced this. It was a much-needed validation! It is interesting that she saw that in my past card reading. I am finding it harder each year to voice my thoughts clearly, but I will continue to write. That is a given. It relaxes me and when I go back and read what I have written sometimes I do not remember some of it and I think when I am older and losing my mind everything will be fresh when I read it.

This is not a book to educate anyone. It is how I feel and what has happened in my life, and I want to share it. I must share it, or I live trapped inside my own body. As you read may you find it is healing some part of you. I am not a professional in any sense. I am just me, well me and there is that little girl Toby that must help me heal as I go back to childhood and sail through life. May my words help you to find solace in your life too. At the very least maybe you will realize we are all screwed up a little and that is perfectly okay now and it should have been then. Be brave and allow yourself to shed bad memories and leave only the good behind. Let the shadow go…. damn it to hell!

MY THOUGHTS

WONDERING

THINKING

IDEAS ROLLING

PONDERING

CONTEMPLATING

WHERE AM I GOING?

TO AND FROM

HERE AND THERE

COMING AND GOING

I'M EVERYWHERE BUT NOWHERE

TOBY

One of my first thoughts that I wrote down when I was around thirteen. It made sense to me about myself. Interesting I always look at it and feel exactly what I try to say inside myself.

To express who I am is ridiculously hard. I have hidden a big part of me inside. There I can protect myself. It is safe. There is where the darkness goes and sits on a shelf. Replace this with happiness. Replace this with love. Replace this with others. Replace it with everything and anything.

If I do not have to show others the dark and hidden side, then they will accept me. Why do I feel the need to suppress all this inside? Why have I allowed the shadow on the wall to win over me? Thus, was born my brave, yet scared, little girl. I call this little girl – Tobika (or Toby as I pen her). I will talk about my shadow, well, Tobika's shadow more times throughout. It helps me to filter through life.

I realized that I lost myself within my own body. When I was young and carefree, I had the world by the tail. I had a formidable family and enjoyed being with everyone. At a crucial point in my life, I shut down. I turned off being the secure little girl. I started to see phantom shadows every night. And these shadows stole me from me.

I, slowly, over a long time have released little bits of this pain. There is so much more that I shelter. She writes about her fears and the unknown in front of her and the turmoil behind her. She is me, yet that little girl is hidden deep and never shows herself to others very often.

She is not happy, but she does try to let me know that it is okay to be myself with her as me. Does that make sense?

I have tried numerous times to start to write what makes me the person I am and would never get past the first page. So today I try again.

Firstly, I have been diagnosed with a Dependant Personality Disorder. What is that??

"Dependent personality disorder (DPD), formerly known as asthenic personality disorder, is a personality disorder that is characterized by a pervasive psychological dependence on other people. This personality disorder is a long-term condition in which people depend on others to meet their emotional and physical needs, with only a minority achieving normal levels of independence."[1]

I am partially in the minority as I have been independent to a degree. But I always feel like I must please others. When others are upset with me, I berate myself for not thinking of their feelings first. I have trouble saying "no" to others and want to see them happy before my own needs of happiness and security are met.

That is me compensating for childhood trauma. That is me trying to make sure Toby is safe. That is me hiding inside my own head.

Recently I realized that when my childhood trauma ended is when I started this disorder. At that time, I had strawberry blonde ringlets in my hair and bounced around everyone giggling. I asked my mom to give me a "Mia Farrow" cut and started wearing more masculine clothing. I enjoyed getting hand me downs from my brothers and wearing t-shirts and jeans. I wanted to blend into the oblivion. I wanted to be in the background, not the forefront. When my sisters and I sang together I would be the harmonizing background and stand behind my oldest sister mostly. I think, also, that my other older sister liked to be behind also as she was subject to some of the same childhood trauma. We experienced some of this together and after the initial trauma stopped, we never spoke about it again.

It's dark now, am I completely safe?
Maybe another blanket or toy onto my bed will do?!
How long have I been laying here awake?
Someone is coming up the stairs, don't make a sound.

Footsteps come to my door; can you hear?
If I stop breathing, then I should be safe!
I think they went away, should I make sure?
Or climb in my closet and just stay awake!

There's the shadow creeping onto my wall
Is it my imagination, have I fallen to sleep?
Shadows can't hurt you, is that true?

But here I lie awake and start to weep.

Cocoon myself within my bed to stay quiet.
No matter how many deterrents I am found.
I pretend to be asleep; did you hear a step?
Will I be safe, don't make a sound!!

Cry inside and hold my breath now.... shh!
It will pass and be over then it's dark.
Shadows on my wall and beside my bed grow
I must gasp for air and shake away the marks.

Does life ever just stop and let me rewind?
Is this my fault and would anyone ever believe?
Each night is the same and I'm out of my mind.
If I could sleep, then I could dream to relieve.

How long can I go without a good night?
Is it okay to breathe, safe to sleep?
I scream from within and then hear my own voice.
Go away! Leave us alone please, please!!

The shadow falls back into the night.
Lights are all on and the shadow then falls
I may be safe, but it has been so long.
Each night the shadow burns still on my wall.

KAL 18/02/26

So, it begins....

Are we living a lie in our lives then? You can be in Heaven and an experience can make it like Hell!

It has been hard to come to terms with myself and with the feeling that I could release that side of me that I have kept hidden. And the sad thing is I have kept it hidden so well that even I hid it from myself.

This little girl in me does not forget the past and every now and then when I am fervently authoring a poem, she pokes her thoughts out and I write as if I was remembering all that happened so exceptionally long ago. Then later when I read, I wonder where that all came from. Sometimes I do not even remember writing it. I have looked over something I know I wrote but did not go back and reread right away and I am amazed and a little proud that I did.

Tobika (Toby) has given me a voice for the pain that I have lived and hid.

Do not get me wrong, I loved my family. I loved being part of a big farming family. I loved growing up with my grandparents in the same house and my other grandparents at Sunday dinner and supper. I loved the fact that our home was the hub of others that came and went and always felt welcomed. No matter what my mom made for supper there was always enough to fill everyone that sat at the table and the extras that just showed up at eating time. We had plenty of food, lots of work to do, many friends and a full house always.

I guess even though that was the joy of my childhood, it also brought the pain of my childhood. I do not have many recollections before the age of 6 or 7. A few memories come through now and then and usually they are good memories. My vivid memories come around the age of eight through to about ten.

We lived in an old farmhouse. My grandparents lived in the lower front of the house, and we lived in the other lower half and the upstairs. My sister and I shared a bedroom. I have blurred memories as to who all were in the other two bedrooms upstairs. My brothers shared a bedroom with "the boarders," that being two queen beds, a double one and a single in one large room. Now, I think my parents still slept upstairs at the beginning, then built on an addition downstairs so that we could have more boarders and they could have privacy downstairs. A bit late if you ask me after 7 children (plus one baby that only lived 10 hours).

This is when my trauma comes in. One of the boarders decided that he should start coming into my sister's and my bedroom. I cannot remember the first time, but I remember the last time. All I remember is after the first time, I stopped sleeping and to this day still have trouble sleeping. How bad can it be right? I was a little girl; my sister was a little older. We did not ask for *his* attention. I remember being afraid to go to bed. I would do anything to stay up later and not have to go to my bedroom. When I did go, I would take every stuffy, every doll, every pillow and blanket, then pile them on top of me then cocoon inside my blankets. I would lie awake as long as possible and then drift in and out of consciousness. And I still cannot just fall asleep at night.

I have had someone tell me that it was not that bad. Others have had it worse. Well true, and yes, we made it out alive. But try and imagine this…. you fall asleep, you jerk awake, you sit up, you look around, you try to calm down.

He is not there anymore, he is not going to wake you up, he is not real to you now. But there is the shadow.

Well, if I am alive, he is there. It is only a shadow on my wall, but he is still there. You would think after fifty years the shadow would fade. It does not. I tell myself I took care of it all by yelling to get out, to leave my sister and me alone, and waking everyone else. I did, but that did not take away that little girl's fear of being awaken to someone else by your bed, in your bed, in your mind, in your body and being the shadow on the wall.

So why am I talking about all this now. I need to cleanse my soul. I need to forgive that little girl for not telling her parents what was happening. I need to try and find an end to a long, horrible secret and start letting life just happen.

I swore I would never tell my parents as this would have caused a wound between families. The boarder was the son of a distant relative and good friend to them. If I told them and they kicked him out then told his parents, who knows where that would have taken the lives of all those other people. I have told some of my story to a few people and some asked 'why not tell your parents now?' No, first I must tell of my anger with my Dad. My anger was that little girl that use to adore her Dad and where was he when she needed him the most?

When I married in 1979, you can see that when my Dad was in the picture, I had a different suppressed even angry look. It took me about a year to notice that myself. And as I was pregnant with my first child in 1980, I finally realized I had been carrying a whole lot of anger because my Dad didn't protect me as a child. And well, he did not. But I finally realized that I was holding that against him. How could he protect what he did not know? So, I apologized for being a rather difficult child and I was forgiven immediately. And no, I did not tell him then. And I never told my mom. I can finally write about it all as now my Mom passed away. Now I can let out of myself that little girl that has desperately tried to get me to talk. I am not talking, but I am writing. I have written all my life in my poetry. Now and then, there is a glimmer of that scared little girl and then someone told me to try and tell them what happened in any way I could.

I sat down and authored a few new poems. I looked back at my dark poetry and decided it should not be included in with other writings. That is where I am today. I need to see the good with the bad. So, I am trying to tell my story including that little girl inside.

With encouragement from others, I will release her somewhat and see what happens as I go. So, to do that I must include some of the poems. You will notice that some have the name TOBY and others KAL. Some are dated and some are not. When they are not dated, I wrote the bulk of them when I was a rebellious teenager.

Just a moment, I must stop and think…. I was a hard to manage teenager – not rebellious. That is settled let us move on. I will warn you that I will jump around a lot as that is what I have always done. My friends laugh at me as I will be talking to them as we drive somewhere and at a blink of the eye, I see something that catches my attention and will lose track of where I was going and what I was saying. Bear with me. My friends and I call that my 'shiny thing attraction' or is that distraction?

"Nobody can go back and start a new beginning, but anyone can start today and make a new ending." ~Maria Robinson

I had no self-respect for myself as a teenager. I think that is because of what had happened when I was so young and then all the other stuff that came after. Again, that would be because I was a lost little girl, and she would show up in my life at various stages and times.

So again, I find myself visualizing myself at the age of 8 or 9. I can see my bedroom and look out the tiny window. I spent a lot of time sitting looking out that window. I can see the big closet that was built of particle board and painted a pinky white. There were two big sliding doors that had four holes each to use to slide them. Inside the full closet you could go from my bedroom to the bedroom beside it. On the closet floor was the piping to bring warm air from the furnace into the rooms. Hardly enough to keep it warm, but big enough to ward off the cold air. Remember this is a big, old farmhouse that was built in the early 1900's. At first it was all open upstairs with only cold air registers strategically placed above where the old wood stoves were downstairs, then the small oil furnace-stoves replaced those. Once a furnace was put in, we slowly had registers put in.

As I turn and look, I see my bed along-side the closet door. My dresser is at the partition wall at my head. My sister's bed is along the outside wall with her dresser by her head at the door. Our door is a bi-fold door that never closes properly. I see the spare dresser loaded with our out of season clothes. There are two chairs and two garbage cans. A multitude of stuffed animals and such around the room. I feel cold remembering this room. There was not a lot of good memories in this room. I was more than happy when given the chance to move into the big room with my sister as the older boys had married and moved out and the boarders had all moved into their own lives. That room was bigger, and I felt better in there than in the other room. The plus was it had an actual door. I have a story about that room and will write about it also. Then as my sister left home, I went to the smaller room beside my original room. I was okay there too as it was only my room.

Back to my room…. I used to love my room with my two sisters when I was little. I have a fond memory of my sister on the bottom bunk and my oldest sister in a single bed on the outside wall. That memory also includes my sister pushing up on my springs and mattress saying "you are going to pee on me!! If you pee on me, I will bop you one." Then bang another kick until I would cry, and our oldest sister would tell her to knock it off and tell me to come sleep with her. In my mind this happened a lot, but I am not sure as I was quite young. I know it was around the time of losing teeth.

Ask me how that memory comes up….

Well, it has to do with me being around five or six, so my older sisters were just at the 'age of maturity.' I vividly remember losing a tooth and putting it under my pillow on the top bunk. The next morning, I got up and looked under my pillow and there was no tooth and no money (it was only a quarter back then). I was extremely disappointed but determined to find one or the other, so I took all my blankets off and search throughout my bed. Then I checked over my sister's. I stood looking at our bunk beds and noticed that the garbage can was positioned on the floor on our head end. Soooooo yep, I started going through all the garbage. I found my tooth but no money. And a 'dead mouse' wrapped in Kleenex. Imagine my sister's embarrassment when I showed up in the kitchen with this 'dead mouse' and told everyone that the tooth fairy was a bad fairy. Then proudly produced this dead mouse holding it up by the tail. My sister ran from the room bawling her eyes out. As she was twelve or thirteen you know where this is going…yes, she was becoming a woman, and I was dangling her used tampon around in the kitchen saying it was a 'gross dead mouse'. I still will say it smelled bad and had a long tail. In hindsight this was one of the reasons she tormented me.

I was not that bad of a kid, I guess. The youngest of seven children. I boast proudly I have been to the east coast of Canada across to the west coast of Canada and almost all the upper states in the United States. I felt honored to travel with my parents and my mom's parents. I was the only one they took with them. I was so loved. Imagine my surprise when much older and sitting around the kitchen table and some of my older siblings said yes that is right, you got to go, and we stayed home. But not because you were a favorite or because you were being honored. It was because they all begged our parents to take me. None of them wanted me to stay behind and torment them. So, in 1967 when I was turning seven, I went to P.E.I. and in 1968 when I was turning eight. I saw the provinces across to BC. I do not care it was great to travel with them and I still say they gave me a wonderful present and that's why I went. Come to think of it in 1968 I was outside trying to help paint the front stoop and had a brush in hand when my mom came around the corner already to leave for BC and she told me to go inside and wash my face and hands as I was going with them. I did and wondered what I was going to wear as I did not pack anything. Oh well, I climbed in the car between my mom and gramma and jumped around excitedly. So, poo on those others saying it was because they made a valiant effort to make them take me. I have great memories from those trips.

Being the youngest of seven has its difficulties. I blended into the background well. My older sisters were allowed to take tap dance lessons, CGIT and 4H. The boys got to play baseball and hockey. I was permitted to take piano lessons but only because the teacher lived across the highway. When she moved, so were the lessons finished. I did take 4H but because my mom was the leader. I joined baseball and thought someone would notice that, but in the ten plus years that I played my mom came to one of my games with my sister (they had to as they needed to pick me up) and my dad made one of my games (only because he was the hired umpire). I always felt that nothing I did was ever good enough and in fact nothing I ever did would make a difference.

Then I would think to myself that I do not want anyone to notice anyway. I ping-ponged in my thoughts as to whether I wanted to get anyone's attention or have everyone's attention. I knew how I could have gotten a lot of attention but then that would mean others would know what I never talked about. God it was hard growing up and keeping things quiet. Believe me I was in trouble for being 'snotty' as my family would call me. Whenever this boarder would come to visit my parents – and yes, he would still come and smirk at me. I, on the other hand, when he was present in the room would take the farthest possible path through the house. If I had to go through the same room, I would take the farthest wall away from where he sat. I developed a sneer that would be one side of my mouth up along with my nose and avoid all eye contact when possible. I remember once he shot up out of the chair he was sitting in and took a step towards me, and I bolted from the room and ran as fast as I could up the stairs and into my room. My parents would shame me for being like this. Sometimes my other siblings would say how 'snotty' I was being.

He got married and they had a couple kids, and they would come to visit my parents. I was older then but now felt I could not say anything that would affect his family. They did not need to hear that from me. His wife was such a nice young woman. I felt sorry for her and when I heard they had split up I was happy for her. She probably never knew anything, and I recently befriended her on Facebook. Not to tell her that her ex-husband and father to her two sons had molested my sister and I, but to try and start a healing inside me. I will never have to see him again, but she was just as much part of his sick sexual stirrings as she was much younger than him. I always felt a bit of comradery with her. And I was relieved when they had sons and not daughters. He had the nerve to try and friend me on Facebook. I blocked him.

WHICH WAY DO I GO FROM HERE?

Which way do I go from here?
I know I was here before.
Though now I seem to forget
How it was I got thru the door.

> Do you remember the way out?
> I'm really getting all disarrayed
> Since I can't figure out myself
> And my memory is all frayed.

Can anyone help me decide?
I thought I would go left – no right.
Maybe just straight ahead
Or I'll head down through the light.

> Doesn't seem hard to figure out
> How to go back and start fresh?
> With each step I take I turn around
> And find out I'm still in this mess.

Which way do I go from here?
I don't want to be here anymore.
Which way do I go from here?
Take me to where I was before.

TOBY

Life was very confusing to me as a little girl. I always felt I was not good enough to others. Whether it be at school, at home, at church, at anywhere. I did not know where exactly I fit in. I never had a true-blue best friend for life. I would flitter around from groups of girls but never develop that lasting friendship most people have. I do stay connected with a few friends from my younger years and some from when I was in high school. The funny thing is mostly I have connected with the guy friends before the girls. Oddly, I felt hesitant to reach out too many of them. Do not get me wrong I do have some close friends now in this stage of my life. But it was not an easy fit. I never did trust myself to just be myself. Then I feel if I let myself go and let them see 'me' they would judge me and then I would not have that friendship anymore.

I can vividly remember times I would just walk out of the farmhouse when I was a young teenager and go to the hay loft and sit there with the family dog and plot my death. Not suicide – how I was going to die. I wanted to die young. I did not want to grow up and have to deal with myself. I had about four or five scenarios that worked, and they made me sad, but I would revisit them there or in my dreams. To this day I have some same dreams and these scenarios come back to haunt me. I must say it is that little girl who wants to voice herself to me. So, I am trying to be open to myself and allow my thoughts to flow down onto paper or into the computer. I have been doing that for a long time with my poetry. Now I am going to put more into getting this out of me.

Over the years, I have tried to bring it out. I would write it down and put it into my poetry papers. I had let little pieces of me come out and tell someone a little bit. If I found rejection, I would tuck it back away. If I felt that the one, I told listened and accepted me, it would help heal a tiny bit of me. I know that a lot of times when I would try and tell anyone a little bit about me, I felt they did not listen. They did not reject it, but I do not know if they did accept it. Sometimes then I would sit down and put it into my poetry or a song.

One of the strange things I have noticed about me over the years is that whenever someone is trying to demean me or not pleased with me, my body shuts down. My soul turns off, my head starts to hurt, my body becomes numb, and my eyes have trouble focusing. It is a strange feeling. I fight to not let anyone notice, but when I finally get alone, I collapse. I used to just drop and cry, but over the years I built a defense mechanism that keeps me going until I can deal with it in private.

I often have others tell me how strong I am. How I manage so much and keep going. I can smile through rough times, believe me on the inside that little girl is throwing a tantrum telling me to let loose. Break the façade and allow others to comfort you. I win usually and do not do any of that. I fight, I smile, I go forward, I console others, I must help them. I think helping them is my way of defending my feelings inside. If someone else can be helped and made to feel better than I can feel some worth for myself.

No one seemed to understand
    What it is I carried inside
I was often left confused
    What it was I did hide.
No matter what it was I did
    That ache was hard to find.
I thought I could suppress it
    That just pushed me over the line.
Whenever I tried to confess
    How difficult it had become,
They would not seem to hear
    How I felt, then they'd shun.
Whenever I came within reach
    Of the solution to this pain,
They seemed to be afraid
    Of maybe sorrow or shame.
But I have come to grips
    With myself and everything.
I'll not turn away now
    With a fear of anything.
But no one can tell me
    About what's all still inside.
I'll be brave and tell you
    About all it is I hide.

TOBY 05/12/96

'Sometimes your joy is the source of your smile, but sometimes your smile can be the source of your joy' – *Thich Nhat Hanh*

As I sit here and think of all the memories that I have hidden for many years, I feel overwhelmed and unsure of what all to write about and how to word it properly. My brain is trying to freeze out my thoughts. It is like a pond that you are watching from a dock, and you can see the chilly air starting to glisten it and slowly it ices up and then you feel an inner cold in your body. That is where I am right now.

Do I keep going or give in and stop? The memories are flashing in front of my eyes, and I am getting tired, and my eyes are not focusing on the screen. I must tell more before it has gone again. What do I do?? It is slowly winning, and I am losing my train of thought. Why can't I just sit down and do this?? Do not let it win? She is trying so hard to keep you motivated…. I must stop, my arms are hurting, my head is buzzing, my eyes are not focusing and be damned if I do not feel like I have not slept in a long time…. wait, that is not unusual as I go through life tired. My mom used to call and say, 'How are you sweetie?" and I would always reply "Fine." Mom would then say, "you wouldn't tell me if you weren't fine, would you?" And I would always say "Probably not mom, would you?" Touche! That was how my mom and I had conversations.

Thinking of my Mom, I know I must stop as I need some time alone with my thoughts and love for my Mom. That little girl will have to wait as I need this more than writing. I miss my Mom a lot. We had such a great connection. She was the rock of our family and now we all must grow up a little more and be our own family's rock.

Again, here I am looking at the computer screen and thinking man how do I put my thoughts together here and tell this story of mine. Really, it is a fraction of my story and I think in the end there will be sideline stories throughout.

I want to revisit my thoughts of my death. It was not a suicide pact with myself or a plan to just die. It was ways in which I could get away from all the pain inside. It was a way to shut down. You know a way to make my life seem less than it was. What I am trying to say is I felt my life was worthless. I know my siblings would say this was not true. They all felt I was the suck of the family. I never felt that way. I felt like I was sometimes invisible. I say this because my thoughts on anything were never asked. When I announced I was engaged and getting married in about 6 months my parents did not even flinch. It was two months later when I asked my mom to come help pick out a bridal gown that she said, 'oh you were serious?' So, my wedding was planned in a flash and there I was getting married. I will come back to this later.

There were many other times I felt invisible. I remember going to play with my cousins while my dad was at a lodge meeting. It was a fun time but soon it was 9 pm and I started watching for him to pull into the laneway. At 10 pm I felt disappointed that here I was, and no one came for me. When 11 pm came the phone finally rang. It was my mom to say my dad was on his way to pick me up. He had forgotten me. He got home and went to bed. After a little bit, my mom asked if I had had fun and my dad asked her why he would know. Yep forgotten. I was invisible. When I got in the car to go home, he said he had totally forgotten me. I just shrugged and told him that is okay. What I did not say was I did not expect anything but to be forgotten. So, no I was not the suck of the family.

I was the baby but only because my baby brother did not live, so only by default. My brother a couple of years older was the favoured child. The golden child in our family. He was never forgotten. He had multiple vehicles to drive. That even after a few write offs. I never had a vehicle to drive. My parents had a car and a truck by the time I was licensed. I had to ask to drive them and quite often would be told that I could not drive either of them as my dad might need it. Okay did you notice I said my dad might need it. My mom did not drive, and they had two vehicles. I could not use either of them because he had not decided if they were going anywhere and which vehicle he would want to drive. If I was my brother, firstly, I would have my own vehicle which my dad had bought for him, or I could just jump into either vehicle and go. This may seem petty but two months prior to my wedding I wanted to go with my friend to visit my soon to be husband and my dad pulled this 'I might need either of the vehicles' reason for not going. I was eighteen, soon to be married and I was being told this lame excuse. Even my mom asked him why. I had asked around 3 pm. I waited patiently until 5 pm and asked again. I waited another hour and a half and asked my mom if she could find out. At this point, my friend called her dad and asked to take their car with a 'yes' so, a cousin said he would give us a ride over there. My dad walked out of the living room and announced I could take the car but had to be home by 9 pm. Figure this out it takes 30 minutes to drive to my fiancé's house so an hour round trip. It was now 7 pm so that would give us an hour there to be home by this ridiculous time of 9 pm. Thanks Dad but my friend's dad is letting us drive their car there and oh by the way, since it is Friday evening, and I don't work this weekend we are going to stay there until Sunday evening now. BYE!! See how I am not the 'favoured' child.

Do not get me started with how my brother only lived off the farm for about three months before he moved back home with his pregnant wife. He had it all set. No rent was charged, no utilities were charged, and he worked so all his money could be used to his own enjoyment. I think no one would be surprised to learn he had a drinking problem and was a heavy smoker!

Once I married, I lived away from home for seven years before my first husband and my family moved home with my parents. And before anyone says well, I should not be upset with my brother living there, I paid half the utilities and bought all our own groceries along with helping with paying the farm taxes each year. My brother and his family now lived in my maternal grampa's house on the farm. (He built a house right on my paternal grampa's farm to be closer to us as he was getting old, and his health was waning.) Both my brother's wife and he worked. My parents paid the taxes. Three times my brother tried to make my family pay rent to him to live with my parents in their house.

My paternal grandparents owned the homestead farm. They had put both my mom and my dad onto the land title when my gramps retired for farming at thirty-five. (He developed a hernia that he refused to see the doctor about) Years after my gramma died in 1969, my grampa had told my dad that he should have him taken off the title as when he passed away it would be easier for Dad and Mom. My Dad and Mom decided to add my brother and his wife on the title as they lived on the farm at that point. So, each person had a quarter of the land title. Later when my Dad had found out he had brain tumors and my Mom had to have surgery, they panicked and had my sister-in-law's lawyer draw up a change that gave my brother and her full title to the land with the exception that the family homestead house remains my Dad and Moms to the day they died. Well, that did not happen.

Also, there was a clause that my brother must give money to each of his siblings to have the full ownership. I think you have figured out by now that no one saw any money from him, and he took it upon himself to move into the homestead house with Mom in 1996. She was not happy and cried when she told me about it. Shortly after she married my stepfather and moved out of the house that had been her home for over 50 years. It was hard on her, but she could not live with my brother and his family. I will say I have never really forgiven him for doing this as my family lived with her and he moved them out, did not give them a choice in the matter and then because he moved them into the other farmhouse made them pay rent. He finally got what he wanted. My sister, had she not passed away a year before mom, was going to sue him for breach of contract and taking advantage of our parents when they were under distress from their impending surgeries. I cry as he burnt many of my childhood memories when he moved in. Gone was my baby book, my baby photos, my special toys, and my own children's baby books and such. That is something that I will never forgive him for, along with some other hidden thoughts of me as a little girl. I will get to that at some point.

Now the farm is less than half the size it once was. All the barns that my father had built were destroyed. Anything of value that was not my brothers was burnt up including a lot of my childhood possessions that my Mom was keeping for me. It hurt to hear of all this, but nothing could be done about it.

I say my family lived there because in 1996 I left for a fresh start and to make a home for my children to come live with me. My husband and I had grown completely apart, and I was slowly shrinking into oblivion. That brings the statement I tell people. I was living in the Garden of Eden, I was one of the second Corinthians, which is down the road from the land of Goshen.

So, I had my 'Eden' and left to find 'Heaven.' 'Hell' had destroyed my 'Eden' and is trying it is best to destroy the 'Heaven' I had found. A lot has happened to my life over the years, and I must make sense of it all to go forward in life. I want to keep 'Heaven' and not let 'Hell' destroy it for me.

But I know that I can make sense quite easily as I try to fix everything for everyone else. I must start fixing me so that I can go forward and keep my Heaven. I am jumping forward again, time to reflect to childhood.

Everyone thought I was a happy child. That is everyone but one of my Dad's cousins. She would have me come to her place and tell me that she can see pain in my eyes that no one else saw. I would dismiss it but at least someone could see 'me.' I enjoyed going to her place although not often enough. At her place it was just me. I did not have to worry about anything. The only drawback was she did not have much for a young child to play with so I used my imagination in her basement and would pretend many adventures.

I do have an early memory of hiding behind my gramma and grampa's oil stove in their side of the living room until the school bus passed our house. I played with the ornaments in the china cabinet until lunch time then crawled out and fell asleep on their couch. Gramma came in and found me there about time for the school bus to be bringing the rest home. I was about six then. She was so worried that no one had missed me going out to catch the bus and that neither grampa nor she had realized I was home earlier. Did I ever get a lot of cookies to eat from gramma and a stern talking to from my parents when they came home? The other kids got an even sterner talking to for not realizing I was not with them.

I also remember that for grade 2 they made us switch school and go to a school that was further away than the school we all had attended prior to that year. Then in grade 3 my Dad made them let us go back to our school closer to us. We were happy to return to our first school.

.

I grow small, I grow big
Within my mind there is no escape
I feel pain, I feel nothing
Is this life real or is it fake?
When I am small no one can see
All the pain bottled up inside
When I am big no one would guess
The truth I've never confide

I am here, I am there
No matter it is always with me
I feel sick, I feel numb
Is this the 'me' everyone sees?
When I am here, I feel empty
As if there is no room inside
When I am there, I don't belong
So, I turn around and hide.

I want to scream, I want to hide
This is what I cover up with smiles
I feel blue, I feel afraid
Is this how everyone else is also?
When I want to scream, I supress my voice
I keep others away from my own pain
When I want to hide, I just keep going
I never want anyone else to feel the same

I'm in pain, I'm not 'fine'
But I won't let go to set me free
I feel inadequate, I feel ill
Put on a smile for everyone to see
When I'm in pain I compensate
Do more for others to mask what I feel
When I'm not 'fine' no one must know
I keep this inside, my lips sealed

I grow small, I am here
I want to scream, I'm in pain
I grow big, I am there
I want to hide, I'm not fine
I feel pain, I feel sick
I feel blue, I feel inadequate,
I feel nothing, I feel numb
I feel afraid, I feel ill.

Within my mind there is no escape
No matter it is always with me
This is what I cover up with smiles
But I won't let go to set me free.
Is this life real or is it fake?
Is this the 'me' everyone sees?
Is this how everyone else is also?
Put on a smile for everyone to see.

When I am small no one can see
When I am here, I feel empty
When I want to scream, I suppress my voice
When I'm in pain I compensate
All the pain bottled up inside
As if there is no room inside
I keep others away from my own pain
Do more for others to mask what I feel

When I am big no one would guess
When I am there, I don't belong
When I want to hide, I just keep going
When I'm not 'fine' no one must know
The truth I've never confide
So, I turn around and hide
I never want anyone else to feel the same
I keep this inside, my lips sealed.

KAL 18/03/01

Like I have said I have flashbacks of my youth. They come and go and never seem to stay long enough to remember them fully. I know I hated getting up in the morning. I was always so tired from not sleeping. I realized that is mostly because I could not sleep well at all. When my mom would yell up the stairs that it was time to get up, I was usually just falling to sleep about that time. I cannot recall many nights where I got into bed and fell immediately to sleep. To be honest I loved going away with my parents as I could fall asleep wherever they went safely knowing that there were people around and I would be on a chair, a couch or under the kitchen table.

When I woke up each morning it was cold in the farmhouse. You could see your breath. I can remember peering out the little bedroom window and think 'I'm still here.' A young girl should not feel like that, should she?! But I did. Do not ask me to give dates or even years as memories come in whatever order they want. I have no control over them. Nor can I just sit down and recall a lot. It seems my memories come mostly in my fitful sleep.

I do remember a dream that came many times when I was at our public school, and I came outside, and there was no one else in the schoolyard. I run inside and can hear others but cannot find them. I run back outside and see some kids in the farthest corner from me. I start to run for them but instead of going towards them, I am floating up. The faster I run, the higher I go. I stop running and start to go down. After many tries, I do start to move towards where the kids are. You can guess it, as I came closer, they moved further away, and I kept trying. Over and over, I would try, yet I never got there. In most dreams I would end my dream by just crashing down to earth in a pile. That is, it. Done. Crazy and I have never tried to make sense of that recurring dream.

Even as I type I become tired. I just want to stop and go lay down. My eyes are not focusing, and my heart feels heavy. I am lost to the world. I am hurting inside and if I push much more I will be gone again. My body feels swollen then feels tiny. I am sitting at my kitchen table and there are kids playing, but I cannot stop yet. My eyes start to hurt, and my anxiousness is mounting. Push Kim, push. Do not give in. Do not stop. Others think I am a strong person. I have never considered myself to be a strong person. Quite the opposite. I look at myself in the mirror (that is scary enough) and I do not see a strong person. To be frank, I see a sad scared little girl. And I do not try to look in the mirror often. My youngest daughter used to watch her reflection in anything she could doing almost everything. Giving a good night hug she would look in the dresser mirror and watch her reflection. Whenever I was trying to make a point to her, I would constantly tell her to look at me not herself. Although I must say I was happy she liked looking at herself. I wish I were.

While going through puberty I tried exercising nude in front of my dresser. I was curious but never happy with my body. That was stolen from me. The satisfaction of looking at yourself and thinking 'hey I look good.' My sister told her Psych teacher about this, and he said sounds normal to me. I know I always hated to get my photo done and when I would see a current photo think to myself how ugly I was. Some say that is normal, but why is that normal? When I look back at a younger me now, I can appreciate that I was not as bad looking as I felt at that time. Even my wedding photos I did not really like. I did not feel like the blushing bride, and I did not think I looked radiant. I wish I did. My second marriage I liked my photos more.

"Unless you learn to face your own shadows, you will continue to see them in others, because the world outside you is only a reflection of the world inside you." – **Unknown.**

Have I taken enough time to make you forget my own trauma? Is it any easier for me after I have written some but not all about it? Have you decided how you feel about me? Has this brought up any worries of your own?

See this is me. I tell a little about me, but I do sugar-coat it and I deflect from the root of my true self. I let Toby out a little and then I cover her up with other stuff, so she does not have to feel anything. I guess I have always been covering her up. First with stuffies and dolls and blankets. Then with life itself. Toby is very much a part of me. She is that little girl. She is trying to maintain her child innocence. Maybe I try to compensate for her, so she doesn't feel like a failure. I take over and make her trauma my reason to go forward. I protect her along with myself. It sounds almost crazy to call my childhood trauma Toby, but it helps me make some sense of life itself. Toby is supposed to be a happy content and cute little girl. I am the one who keeps her safe. I am the one who lets her tell a little bit at a time. She is not real, but she is. She is me before I was molested. (*It is so hard to say that aloud*). She is me before I lost my innocence. She is me before

I stopped loving myself. Toby is me. I do not have multi personalities, I have a hidden source of unhappiness and yet I do not despise having Toby. And I am slowly letting go of that little traumatized girl. It is not easy to be fragile. I am not use to that feeling. It makes me feel a lot of fright. I cannot control myself if I am not happy and strong. Does that make sense to you?

Back to my childhood. To say it was an unhappy one would be a lie. To say it was the best childhood anyone could ever wish for, again, a lie. I would say it was great as to what almost everyone saw. I was immensely proud to be part of my family. I would boast about how terrific my parents were and how great times we had also. And that was true. No one wants to bring a dark cloud into the story of a family. No one wants to hear that story. People want to hear the good stuff from that era. Nowadays people look for the bad and do not want to hear about the good stuff. At least it seems this way. Growing up in the 60's and 70's was a great time. I do not think I would want to be a kid now. It is way too fast. Life is passing us all by and the future is coming at us all at the speed of light.

Life was slower for my childhood. The nights became long, and I tried my best to sleep, but inevitably sleep only came after a much toss and turn event. Just when I would finally find sleep the sun would creep up and the house would come alive again. I do not remember sleeping well at home. As I have already said, I do remember going with my parents to family gatherings or friend's homes and there I would be sleeping like a baby anywhere I could. I remember sleeping on couches, chairs, floors, beds, stair steps. What I never remember is getting home and into my own bed. I guess I could say if I fell asleep away from home I could be picked up, carried in and out, put into my bed and then I could sleep. My body would relax if it were not my bed so I could get into a deep sleep. That rings true today also as I can start to watch a show and then fall asleep on the couch. My husband leaves me there as he knows I am sleeping. I also can fall asleep easier when he is watching a show late at night in our bed and I know he is awake and watching over me. I know many nights I would sit at my bedroom window and stare out at the pole light in the middle of the yard. I would imagine myself somewhere else. I would believe I was supposed to be somewhere else. I would think I was adopted. And to be honest I really believed it. Friends of my mom's would tell me that I just appeared one day. They said they saw my mom in August and had no idea that she could be pregnant and then saw us in September and there I was. I, also, am probably the only one of my siblings without any names from ancestors. My sister would say that she got to pick my names. That is crazy. It is like my parents really did not want me or expect me so let us let our ten-year-old name her. Questions?????? Yep, I have a few. Other than now I am seeing a familiar resemblance to some of my relatives. Or was I one of my relative's oops?!?!?!? Hey things like that happened back then.

I used to think – Is this why no one noticed when I changed? Did they not see the turmoil inside my head? I know I did not say anything, but did no one not see me change? The happy, little girl got her beautiful blond curly hair all chopped off? No one? Was I by myself? Was I part of my family? Questions, many questions. It happened to my other sister too, does she feel like me? Should I have talked to her? Should I have told my parents what happened? Should I have just told my brothers and let them deal with *him?* I was so confused, hurt, afraid, lonely, damaged, insecure, and alone. Do not confuse loneliness with alone! I knew at an early age that the two were totally different.

I have stood in a crowd of people and still been alone. I have participated with a group of others and been lonely. The two feelings although similar created a different feeling within me as a little girl. Take a minute for yourself and think have you been with a group of friends, they are all happy, they are having a fun time and there you are with a feeling of standing just slightly out of that familiar circle. You see them, you hear them and yet you just know none of them would notice if you left. Then can you also remember a time that you are amongst a group of people and even though you try to belong you feel that little unhappy feeling that makes you feel so blue and lonely. It is a different kind of lonely and alone.

Some people will never have to feel both of those. They are the lucky ones. This little younger version of me, well she feels both. Not always together, but definitely all the time she has at least one of those holding her captive. I am afraid of letting her go, letting her free, letting her shout out who she is and why, letting her become just a time in my life and not a separate entity. Do I hold her captive too? Have I been wrong in protecting her? I get confused and wonder if I should start from the beginning and let out exactly how things felt and how they happened. And once I do let her free can I let her go? I feel she is a part of me I need just to be me now.

Over the years I have tried on various occasions to talk about my life and each time I tell a little more. It helps me to release a little of myself and get on track with my current life. It is not easy to keep her inside, not is it easy to talk about it to anyone. But now is the time to let myself start to heal. Maybe this will help me get stronger health wise today. Nothing is for certain and who knows this may also push me over the top and I will lose myself, or at least what I think is myself. Maybe I won't like my new self. I will finally be myself. Oh, it is a slippery slope sometimes. Okay I will go forward, I think. Yes, I must as I need to see who I really am. I sure hope my family like me when I have finally shed the protective seal I have placed over that part of my life.

Over the years I have tried many separate times to talk about my past. I have consoled other women who have been traumatized and gave them my compassionate ear. I would tell a little of what happened to me and let them know they were not alone and that over time and with the help of professionals they can overcome some of the hurt inside. And before you wonder no, I never investigated letting a professional into my own pain. Well, I did a few times but never felt comfortable enough to take it anywhere. I kept telling myself that I was all right because I managed it all myself when I was ten years old. I did manage it, didn't I?

Once I talked to a mental health person and opened a door about something else that happened as a child and that did not go as planned. She could not help me, she at least said she could not. It was out of her spectre. So, my GP referred me to a psychiatrist, and I met with a local one. Do you know he gave only twenty minutes for a first time visit and did not even let me start with why I wanted to see him in the first place? He talked for the first ten minutes then asked a couple mundane questions he could have found out in my doctor's referral. I opened my mouth to ask him something and he stood up and said, "Thanks for coming in, my secretary can book you in for another visit if you feel you need one". **If I feel I need one???** Well, no I do not feel I need one, I know I need one, but I did not feel it was with him. So, I walked away and decided to hole up again as that did not go as planned. I did not release anything I needed to. So, I tucked that away again and did not open up to anyone more for a bit.

I am sure my first traumatic experience lined up all future traumatic experiences. Yes, there were more than I started with. Unfortunately, that is more than I care to open up about, but I can't write my story and leave out them also. Do not fret though there are not too many. And I managed them like I managed my life.

But I will get to them sometime and hopefully before I bore the *crap* out of everyone, including myself.

Let us go back to square one. I was the youngest of seven. My oldest brother was fourteen when I came along. I was spoiled – yes. I was daddy's little girl. I was called *'toots'* by my mom, *Shirley Temple* by some, *trouble* by others, *annoying* by a few and **sucky** by siblings. My older brothers' friends all would bring treats for me and make me feel special. My parent's friends all loved me and always made me feel special too. I loved the attention. My older siblings would carry me everywhere and speak for me. My mom would joke and say she didn't even know if I could walk before, I was five because everyone carried me around. If I did something wrong, one of my siblings would swoop in and tell my parents that they had me. Maybe I don't remember my early years because they were good. Maybe you only remember once the 'bad' happens. How many other children go through this type of memory loss? Do you not remember when things are good? Do you forget the good if bad happens? Questions I have wanted to ask someone professional? Maybe one day I will get that answer. Even with all this I was not the favoured child and that is okay as it is easier to hide from being noticed.

Okay our house was the hub of our small farming community. My family was in great regard by all. Everyone loved my parents. They were very community involved. Farmers came by for haircuts by my mom. My mom could do almost anything. We had a small dairy farm and my parents and all of us kids as we became capable worked off the farm in tobacco. It was the best way to make a lot of money in a short time. My paternal grandparents lived in the other part of the farmhouse. They were there almost always. They covered as babysitters, and we grew up knowing a lot about family by having them nearby. I loved spending time with my gramma. I do remember telling her many times about how much I loved her, and I would just die if she ever died. She always laughed and told me that I would live long after her and that is the way life was to be. She died when I was nine. Another sadness I have inside. Her death devastated me. She was my gramma. She was always there to make me feel better. She loved me no matter what. She never got angry or judged any of us kids. It took me until I was twelve to mourn her and actually cry my eyes out. And I did not do that until I was at camp away from everyone.

Hmmmm? You know I have tried to never break down in front of anyone. I know when I was going through all my trauma, I would cry a lot at the drop of a hat. I would become sullen in an instance. And the reaction I received from my siblings was one of calling me names like 'sucky baby,' 'cry baby', 'immature child', 'brat', 'little froggy child', 'bullfrog Pete' and more. I remember them all saying along with their friends and older cousins that I just ruin everything because I cry all the time. I decided a long time ago that I would not give anyone the pleasure of seeing me cry again. My mom would send me into the haymow to see what the older siblings, cousins and friends were doing I would see and hear a lot. Experimental sexual stuff. Farm life as I have been told. The stories each of us have growing up is more beneficial than any relationship or sex book on the market.

I started realizing I did not fit into my family. And I would sit and daydream wondering if I was a lost child, placed into a family that was not mine. I would wonder what I would be like if I lived somewhere else. What would my life have been like if I had not been born into my family?

A redeeming feature in our household was my gramps who would be at our kitchen door separating our kitchens whenever someone was hurting me or teasing me. He would fly through the door and stand in front of me saying 'stop aggravating this child!!' Well, maybe he was not my redeeming feature, but it felt good to have someone in my corner. My gramma was so soft and loving, at least that is what I say. Gramps and gramma were the best.

The back story on my grampa and gramma and why they slept in separate beds I learned much later in life. Another story to tell. But to this day the skeletons and shadows that came out of our little farmhouse remain many. When I was young my gramps told me that the original owners of the house I grew up in, left after they had built the current house. When my grampa bought the land, he had disposed of the homestead home that was originally a little further into the farm and on the top of the worm hill. Worm hill because that is where we dug for fishing worms and where the septic system drained when high. Another laughable story. Gramma and gramps had to sod the sand around the house. They spent years adding straw and grass seed to keep the sand from blowing away.

Focus, focus, focus. Now where was I…. oh, ha, holding in my inner self. Like I have said I have taken to calling her Toby. I have always loved that name since I had heard the name Tatum O'Neil. So, I made my pen name Tobika Annette Teresa Ulaine Michaels – TATUM. And this is how Toby was born. As I may have already said later in life, I changed my pen name to KAL as in my initials. I had left my marriage and moved on. My husband now convinced me that I should close that chapter in my life, and he was right. But I still need to purge that time in my life to move forward. The mind needs to let go, and the soul need to heal. Toby needs to voice herself and help close that horrible time in her life. So, continue if you are still with me, let us get going.

Going back to around five to seven. I was so tiny that my oldest sister would have me run into her arms, but we would do gymnastic moves. She would flip me down then high over her head and around her back and through her legs. Then when we were all through, she would grab my one ankle and wrist and she would fly me all over the kitchen and appliances. I wished I could be a bird and fly out and away. She never dropped me and never hit anything. I loved that and then that stopped as she went to nursing college and started dating. You know got a life. Her boyfriends always loved me – and I told her that constantly. I was in love with each one of them.

IF I COULD BE

If I could be a bird on winged flight,
I'd take to the skies through the night.
My journey would end when I found you
And down I'd come from the path I flew.
I'd then want to be yours till the end of time
Flying together would be suit me fine.
I will always belong right by your side.
Ah, but if I were a bird and could fly.

TOBY 10/10/96

Again, though there is a block of about the same time my trauma took place. I do not remember so much happy times. I do remember being in trouble though. So, if you have a child that was once funny and happy and suddenly, they change please sit down and have a chat often with them. You do not have to make them tell you anything but reassure them that you love them and that you will listen to anything they want to ask about or talk about. I honestly cannot say if anyone tried to ask me or talk to me back then, but I do not think so. Oh yes, they noticed a definite change in my demeanor. That is why I would get in trouble. For my insolence and defiance. And that was especially when my 'shadow' made itself present on my bedroom wall, in my nightmares or in person. Makes you wonder how no one could see that. Did my sister change too? I cannot say I saw much of a change. As she was seven years older than me, she was starting to date and such. She had a regular boyfriend that she dated for many years. She went off to nursing college a few years later also. But she returned home before she moved out to Alberta for a while where she married and started her family. I was so young and dealing with my own trauma that I did not notice a big change other than she stopped 'aggravating this child'. She became a nicer sister that is for sure, but that could just be because she had matured.

I do remember because of photos that I sat on my dad's lap regularly when I was little and would eat with him. My mom said I was always finishing my food and wanting to sit with dad and eat his too. One story they use to tell was at supper one night I refused to eat in the highchair, so when dad sat down, he took me. I still refused to eat. I was crying and pointing throughout the meal. Now back then my mom put everything in bowls on the table. They offered everything to me, and I kept pushing it away. In desperation mom started putting everything in front of me. I was hungry and I knew what I wanted. Green beans on vanilla ice cream. And she said I ate two helpings of it. I never asked for it again, but they all laughed at my weird craving. Just something I know happened before I was eight.

I have been told when I was around three or four, I was helping my mom wash dishes and my next older brother came along and started teasing me, so I picked up a butcher's knife and turned around and stabbed it about ½" into the top of his skull. Did not do any damage but that was probably the most violent thing I have ever done. I, of course, do not remember this but trust the story happened. And as to really how far is in question. One of my brothers told me it was lodged into his skull, and he had to be taken to the hospital. My sisters have always said it was not really in his head but that I had gotten my message across for him to back off.

Have I sidelined enough around my main story? I have been told that I am good at that. Getting the conversation changed from something I do not wish to speak about. I would much rather hear someone else talk and let me help them. Most of the reason I took a dark road that I had to live through. Everything for a reason – right. Sometimes though that reason lays deep, so deep, within you that it takes a lot of time to get it all out. Believe me I always look for the reasons my life takes turns and has many stops. My dark places get a tiny light and I try fervently to cover it all up and get others to depend on me, so I do not have to confront my own obstacles. It has been a long, hard road from being that little girl watching the shadows on the wall and feeling so much sadness in her heart. Our lives are controlled by many things.

I remember my childhood trauma, but I desperately try to not think or dwell there. I feel sick when I do. As I write this, my head is throbbing, my eyes are becoming less focused. I have developed a horrible pain in my left jawbone. My arms are not functioning properly as my fingers try and get as much typed in before I cannot go on today.

When I grow up, I will be in control
When I grow up, I won't hurt anyone
Wait a second for me to think more
Wait a second for me not to run
I want to just go far away
I want to stay here without fear
Hold on now as I make sure
Hold on now as the coast clears

Will I ever feel safe and confident?
Will I ever trust others ever again?
Put away my dolls and toys under my bed
Put away my happiness and learn to defend
There are reasons I stay up late
There are reasons I don't want to sleep
Just one person takes away your life
Just one person can make you weep

As I turn away from the mirror
As I turn away from things I love
To compensate my inner insecurity
To compensate I don't gather, I shove
Will time fade away the memory?
Will time fade the terror, the pain?
I hang my head and try to forget
I hang my head and think of the shame

Do I wish ill on those who hurt me?
Do I wish I didn't carry this fright?
I'm trying hard each and every day
I'm trying hard not to fade from sight
I hope I have forgiven and carried on
I hope I have overcome my deepest pain
How do I make sense from all of this?
How do I make choices that don't wane?

I will try hard to look forward today
I will try hard to not think I'm at fault
The day may be longer than I like
The day may make me think of this assault
I put away all the thoughts for today
I put away all pain until tonight
This is the hardest part of each day
This is the way I stand up and fight

KAL 15/03/02

I have such a need for the comfort of control, yet I let so many others control my days. What do people see when they see me? Do they know me? Do they love me? Are they happy to see me? Have I done enough for them?

I think 'me' as a little girl left behind some of her own thoughts and concerns. She rebelled a little. She stopped caring for herself. She started listening to others and their problems. She never stopped long enough to find true friendship. She bounced from friend groups to friend groups and back again. She felt she had nothing in common with anyone very much. Maybe she looked for someone that needed her to help them, so she didn't have to think about herself.

I will revisit these thoughts many times. I know the answers mostly myself. I do not need confirmation from anyone to know some of my life's questions answers. Have I confused you enough to make you put my story down and decide 'man, she is screwed up and I just cannot follow her thoughts'! Do not worry I have put it away for over 50 years now. No judgment here. Or you cannot go on because you too have an important storyline in yourself. If you do, please, start to put it into some sense and let your oppressed little person have their say. It does help as it lets you rid yourself of the demons and shadows that make living each day happily so hard. I gave my troubled soul a name so I could look at what happened to her then try and help.

I am going to try and relate some of the pain that my shadow brought into my life, and I cannot say it will make a lot of sense. To me it will, and it will also release what happened out into the universe and out of my scared little girl trapped inside my soul.

Okay, you should get a drink and snack so you can relax. Are you reading this out on your patio? That is how I think of it. You, my reader, sitting back on your chaise lounge enjoying a peaceful, warm day. The sun is shining, and the birds are chirping. You have a delicious fruit drink sitting in a pitcher and your glass is half empty already. The hummingbirds are flitting from flower to flower. Your faithful dog or cat is curled up sleeping at your feet and you have no distraction right there in your safe and happy environment.

Or you are in a dark place as I have been and that is okay. I will be here for you. Keep reading and I will take you away from that, if only for a moment in time.

My first recollection….

I am just warm and safe laying in my single bunk bed, now on the floor instead of above my sister. I had a wonderful day playing outside in the big sand hole that grampa and dad put in beside the centre well and pole light. It was a safe place to play. Grampa and gramma could watch me play from their kitchen window and I saw everyone come and go in our laneway. I can almost smell the flowers planted around the house. The lily of the valley, the lilacs, the jack in the pulpits, so many aromas in the air. The garden is growing so every time the wind blows, I can hear the rustle of the corn plants and such. I am too young to help with much, so I get to watch a lot. My bed is nice and comfortable. I drift off into a deep sleep. I am drifting into dream; I will think it was probably about running around carefree with my siblings. Maybe building a chair fort outside using every blanket, pillow, and chair from the house. My mom was so patient with us. I would be princess of the castle, I am sure. The world is all mine.

…. Why is it getting so dark in the castle? What am I feeling? I know I was standing at the top of the castle and the wind was blowing in my long, blonde hair. Why is someone touching my hair? The wind does not feel like that.

I can hear someone whispering my name. Why are they whispering? Someone is touching my body. Why would they do that? I am afraid to open my eyes as my dream disappears with black storm clouds ripping all the blankets into the air and chairs are disappearing as they tumble all over the place and everyone is getting farther and farther away. I am getting so small in my mind, and I feel incredibly sad and afraid. I try to roll away and curl into the fetal position holding my blanket over my head. Is that enough to make the whisper go away? I peek out from my blanket and there is a dark figure kneeling at my little bed, and I can see a large shadow on the wall cast from the pole light outside. I tremble and want to scream. I hold my breath hoping that will be enough to make the shadow get smaller and leave. But it does not, so I stay as still as I could, almost like a corpse on a morgue table. The dark figure remains. I hear a couple of my brothers coming upstairs to bed. Should I scream? If I scream, will they come to my rescue? No, I am too embarrassed to scream. I am not sure if anyone would believe me. I open my eyes a little and the shadow is not there. So, okay I can fall asleep again. I toss a little, I turn a lot. Sleep is not happening, so I count sheep. I think I got to about fifty and started to drift away. Okay let us find my castle again.

Wait the clouds are coming in again, little princess. So, I know I grabbed my blankets and held on. The shadow grows on my wall again and I can feel someone getting close to me again. My blankets are tugged, and I try to hold on. I keep grabbing at them tighter, but they get torn from my tiny fingers. I am scared! Why am I all alone? In a house full of people, I feel so alone! I hear the threat voiced by the shadow to keep quiet or I will get hurt. But I am hurting right now anyway. A hand goes over my mouth, and I try to gag from the smell, but the hand stays there. I feel my nightgown being lifted from my bottom and my underwear is pushed down away from my bottom end. What is happening? I feel a sharp pain in my crotch. And try to pull away but I am still being held down by the dark figure. My eyes search the darkness and all I can see is that shadow on the wall. Tears fall from my eyes. I can only hope my tears will make me feel better. After that I just lay still and hope I can take my mind away. Think about something! Try to put yourself somewhere else.

All I know is suddenly I am waking up and the sun is shining outside. It is morning. I do not remember falling to sleep though. I sit up in bed and look around. I see my sister sleeping in her bed. I see my toys on the floor. I lean over and look under my bed to make sure there is nothing there. Nope all clear. I get out of bed and try to make sense of my night. I get dressed and head downstairs. I slide onto the table bench and have a piece of toast. Most of the household have gotten up already and gone to work or outside working on the farm. I try to figure out how to tell my mom how I am feeling and what happened but then I hear the shadow's threat. It hangs over my head like a guillotine. If I say something terrible things will happen. I do not want to be the reason they do so I sit there and quietly eat my toast. No one even notices me being quiet. So, I fade away from the table and go outside to talk to the dog. At least the dog licks my face, so I know he is listening to me. He sees me!

This was the start of my trauma. The shadow is now there in my nightmares. Only this nightmare was real. I hear the threat whenever I think about shouting out and asking for protection. I, also, know my parents have boarders to help with the bills. It is not going to make anyone rich, but at least we can live. As children, we started working as soon as we could off the farm. Until we became eighteen and finished school all our monies go into the family pot. Mom and dad would get whatever we needed so we did not care about putting all our money there. We were poor farmers, but what we lacked in money was made up in love. At least the love of family is steady. Or is it? There lies another trauma. A dirty little trauma again…. later when I find the words.

I prayed fervently to change how I felt. I loved going to church every Sunday with my parents and siblings. It was a safe place and while others listened to the minister, I was asking God to grant me a big favour. There are those who would say He didn't listen, but I believe He did, and He equipped me with enough bravery to finally do something myself. At least, that is my thought. I do wish it had been sooner. I never blamed God for anything, I blamed the dark, evil shadow.

As I lay me down to sleep
   I pray to God my sanity to keep
      If I should lose it before I wake
         Please grab a hold and give me a shake
            If I should stay sane another day
               Please say a prayer and show me the way.

          TOBY   **10/09/95**

Before you say to yourself, 'why didn't I tell my mom and dad?' I knew the threat was real. It was real because I believed it. What was the threat exactly? That did not matter but bodily harm to me and to my sister was voiced. Also, the threat that no one would believe us – that came after the first few times, and we had not said anything. And no, my sister and I did not talk about it. Through embarrassment, possible harm from the boarder to us and maybe to others, disbelief that this was really happening to us, worry that we would be blamed, the loss of the boarder's rent money to help with farm costs, and so much more. I cannot put my finger on all the reasons as some come to me while I relive my nightmare and write about it. Since my sister and I never talked about it, I only assume her reasons were like mine. Maybe one day when we are sitting around enjoying life we will return to the nightmare and the shadow on the wall. I do not see that happening as we live 3,000 miles apart.

That brings up more distress for me as I do not want to go back home anymore. I have gone back on a few occasions, but sometimes I cannot come for these reasons and sometimes I cannot because I know the shadow will loom there. I am happy being so far away from where that little girl locked herself up in my soul. I continued and grew, but she has stayed hidden deep inside me. I only told two people up to when I had turned forty. My two husbands as I felt they deserved to know why I may show a few quirks in my life. Both were great with the news, but I felt my first husband did not know how to deal with it, so it did not come up again. I only told him after I spent a whole night crying about the incident with my dad when I was pregnant. And maybe the trauma wasn't the main subject as was why I had been so angry with my dad. I cannot fault him though as he never managed any stress. I did. The few times I asked for his help with a tricky thing he had panic attacks, so I never shared stressful situations with him after that.

My second husband has been a trouper. He is incredibly supportive and always wants to know what is happening so he, too, can help. I thank God for both as they are two different men. My first husband was a wonderful father for my four children. But as they matured, he fell back a little and I believe that was because he felt they were so far past where he was. You see he never finished school and always felt less of a person – which he was not. I think the one reason our marriage ended is because I was starting to hear that little girl a bit. She came out in my poetry, and I drew back which caused my husband to draw back. We went our separate ways. Plain and simple. I needed to leave the home we lived in as it was my childhood home, and I could feel the change in me. He did not want any change and did not know what to do. So, I accepted a job transfer from Ontario to British Columbia. This is where I started to feel my heaven and my hell. Living in Eden was like keeping this inside part of me buried and even though I was slowly feeling her, I could not let her exist. I had to stay protected as that *damn* shadow was still there on the wall. I felt it but did not recognize that as my unhappiness. So, I left. I left my husband. I left my childhood home. I left my children with their dad with the agreement that they would come to me at the end of the school year. Guess what – that did not happen. Well did not happen then, at least.

CAN'T SEEM

What is it I thought about?
Do you remember what it was?
Can't seem to remember last night
My eyes are blurred my mind's lost
Was it you I talked to last night?
Or did I just imagine your voice?
Can't seem to think clearly mow.
But you said I had made my choice.

Where did I go, it's just not clear?
And when did I get back here?
Can't seem to get a grasp on it.
What did I say when I was there?
Who was it I was with if not you?
Wasn't it you that I had found?
Can't seem to feel good about it all.
All that's left is to listen to no sound!

KAL & BUB 09/05/04

That is another story in my life. Isn't it funny how when we sit down, we find our lives had many different sub stories that make you who you are and where you are? The chance that a different decision could have changed your life dramatically. I have always held onto the belief that everything happens for a reason. And I have always held back my feelings since I can remember. Maybe my childhood trauma is why. Maybe events after are why. Maybe I was always deemed to be like this. Did God create all these obstacles to place me exactly where I am sitting in front of my computer typing away as quick as I can???? I so hope and this will rid me of all the *crap* I have held inside all these years. I also hope when anyone reads this it will become therapeutic for them also. It does help to release pent up anxiety, anger, hatred – anything you may hold inside that needs to be said. At least once!

The trauma happened many times over about 2 years. My sister was not always home as she worked in tobacco at my uncle's farm and stayed there for a couple months. I dreaded being alone at night. I would stay up as late as possible. I would get into trouble for going up and down stairs after I went to bed. I would use as many excuses as possible to not have to go back to my room. You know, if you have a child doing the same thing, investigate why? It may just be they are naturally a roamer, but they may be indirectly trying to tell you something. Other than some fleeting memories during this time I think I blacked out all the time my bedroom would become a war zone for me. The shadow came and went. On occasion it did not come to my bed. And on occasions it came only to my bed. But mostly he was at both our beds.

I can remember one time; I came awake with his penis in my hand. I would try and pull my small hand away, but he would grab my arm and threaten me. At least it was not near my crotch I thought. So, I laid stiff straight and forced my eyes closed and waited for him to withdraw from my bedroom. I cried into my pillow each time regardless of what would happen.

Shortly before I took the courage to yell at him, I had found my sister's 'you are maturing' books. I read what I could at ten. Then there was a new horror. Would my sister or I become pregnant with his child? Would I be able to hide that, if so? I would have nightmares where I would be happily riding my bike around the yard and then I would look down and my stomach would grow. It would grow and grow and suddenly I would be falling off my bike. I would feel intense pain and my stomach would explode and miniature copies of the shadow would immerge from my stomach and then I would die. I would have the thought in my mind that I had to do something or there would be too many shadows in the world and no little girl would be safe. It took more of these nightmares before I got that courage to yell at him. It was well thought out. I was more afraid of what could happen, then what had happened. So, to protect my sister and me I would get brave.

I sat in my bed that night with my clothes on and stuffiest completely making a wall then blankets upon blankets around me. I had pushed my bed up to the closet wall so that I had only one side available. I waited and waited. I did this for quite a few nights before our door slid open and the shadow approached my sister's bed. She was in a deep sleep as she had been snoring a little. He had only just reached her bed and I yelled! I yelled and I threatened, and I yelled some more. He shrunk away from her bed, and he disappeared into the hallway. Suddenly, lights came on in my brothers' room and the hallway. All the guys stumbled out of their beds into the hall and looked around including that boarder. My sister rolled over and rubbed her eyes telling me to go to sleep. I do not know if she had been aware or what, I did not ask and never did all these years. My one brother came to our room and asked if I was okay and I recall saying, "I will be from now on." Had I defeated him??? Had this worked. I know for that time being it did, but the shadow remains there. Shortly after that he moved out. I felt redeemed.

Although I had taken him out of the equation, I would still wake up and see the shadow and have nightmares it would happen again. No child should be so scared to live. I know I changed. I know I now suspected any movement in the house to be that of the shadow returning. I wasn't spontaneous anymore. I lacked commitment to do things I used to life to do. I loved singing and would belt out songs with my Dad or my sisters before. Now they had to coax me, and I would shrink behind them. My Dad had a beautiful voice and I used to sing with him everywhere. My favourite with him was 'Try a little Kindness' by Glenn Campbell. After this happened, I was hard pressed to sing it as I did not feel kindness at that point. I only wished I had thought of recording it with Dad so I could hear him singing again. I have one recording of him singing and I cherish it to this day.

The only problem after that is for almost two years I lived with that fear and my sleeping was never the same again. I still cannot sleep at night. Yes, more reasons have added onto why, but I know the shadow looms still. How do I know? Well about a year after this all took place I jolted from a nightmare. I was walking up to my school and some of my friends were playing in the front. As I approached, they all turned around and pointed at me, laughing and jeering. I could see their faces coming up close and then falling back. Their laughter and jeers stung my eyes into crying. I looked down and there was the shadow attached to me and laughing also. In my nightmare I thrashed my arms hitting at the shadow and it would not go away it was attached to my body and holding on tight. I ran and ran towards home from school. I made it to the corner, and it was still there. I ran past cars going down the road. I ran to the next corner to turn towards home and there it was still. I ran till I reached my home, and I could not open the porch door. It was locked or stuck. It would not let me in, and the shadow was enveloping me. I cried out and then finally I woke up. I was drenched in sweat and suddenly cold. I wrapped my blankets around me, and I think that is when I stopped sleeping in my bed. What I mean is I would lie on top of the blankets with a housecoat or little blanket over me. I needed to know I could get away from being inside my blankets and away from the shadow nightmare. I did not tell anyone about this nightmare. Actually, this is the first time I have put it into words and typed it out. I have not spoken of it to anyone. It frightened me so much and right now I feel an urge to stop writing as my arms are aching, my eyes are blurring, and my body is so tense I am sure if anyone came up to me, I'd jump out of my skin. My grandson is quietly playing with his toys and as I typed faster and faster, he stopped and watched me. Did the shadow fly out of my body, and he saw it? Am I making a lot of noise typing? Does he see that I have hung my head and tears are starting? I must stop as I cannot focus right now. I need to step back and relax a little as my back muscles are so tense that my head is pounding. I can only hope this acts as a release. Time will tell.

I honestly hate going to bed as that is when the mind starts wandering and wondering. Dreams become repeated nightmares. Any dream, good or bad, can start to weigh on your mind when repeated over and over.

Darkness falls now over the blue sky
    I'm up, I'm down, I don't know why.
The light is gone from within my little room
    My body is in pain way too soon

Into the night I want to just scream
    No one listens or knows what I mean
I falter, I fight, I then lose all control
    No matter what I do, it eats at my soul

Creeping into the hours of the early morn
    I am so tired now, I am so forlorn
Sleep stays away and I try to count sheep
    I lay wide awake; patience I can't keep

I've tossed and turned; my pillow is on the floor
    I pace back and forth and look out my door
Tomorrow is here now and I'm still wide awake
    The pain is high; it is just too much to take

Tonight, I will try again to see if I can lay down

I have to get some sleep; here to do that now
My headache increases and the day is going slow
Will I sleep, will I rest, I need to know?

KAL 17/05/22

If anyone thinks writing is easy, they need to try. My grandson is seven now and there is one more at nine months old. I took a break. A long break. No longer living in the house with the kids, my husband and I have bought our retirement – a big travel trailer with a slide. We have it parked in front of the garage and are living in it. So much smaller than the house, but now the kids have privacy and we do too. We have a small bedroom that is mostly our queen bed, but we sleep better as we have no electronics in it. We seem to sleep better with a smaller room, well I know I do. There is no room for shadows on the wall also. We have ample space for the kitchen, living room and dining area. Two double bunk beds for guests along with a fold down couch and table that drops down to a sleeping area if needed. A full bathroom with shower. It is cozy.

Okay let us back track and see if we can form a solid thought wave.

I cannot remember a lot of things as a preteen except the turmoil of how I felt. So much to remember and too much to share at that time with anyone. I did not trust many to share how I felt and so many times I was labelled as being slightly rude when I had to be around anyone that made me uncomfortable. Life continued and I guess so did I. I grew up, I dated a lot, I worked, I partied, I married, I had kids, I moved, I divorced, I remarried for life, I lost myself, I lost my job, I even went to jail. Yes, never thought I would be there and neither did anyone I met there. I was made an example of - I am sure, nevertheless there I was. It has given me this start to rid myself of the pain I carry.

That part will come later.

I found out who were friends, who were not, who never were or will be and who were, and I didn't even know it. As much as I would like to think I knew who I was then I really do not think I did. I am still working on that. I went from a happy child to a lost child extremely fast. The mask I wore was more for me than for others. I did not want to talk about it. I did not want anyone to ask questions. I think my body gave me the reflex of whenever anyone talks for any length of time, it shuts down. I used to sit in meetings and force myself to stay focused and awake. Kind of like a defense reaction. Just like when he would enter the room. If I just did not move and stayed quiet, I would be okay. Once it ended, I could not sleep when I was supposed to and had a lot of difficulty being awake to the world when I should.

I know I started then overcompensating for my lack of confidence by being involved with others. I could not do enough or be busy helping others enough. I know now that is where my downfall started. It also is when I started feeling what others were without them telling me. Today I know I am an empath. I can be in a store and feeling okay and just like a flash of lightning I can have such a sense of dread or just outright sickness. Maybe I always have known but only lately have I realized this.

'Who am I?' is something I think of often.
'Can I be different?' I always wonder.
When I think out loud, I am never sure.
When I am quiet it's loud as thunder.

It's never been easy to fit in my life
I'm not sure but try to look ahead.?'
My memory brings up events to me
Feeling a lot of pressure in my head.

I'm trying to figure out the little girl
Is she the one who keeps me safe?
Is she the one who holds me back?
I like to think but that keeps me awake.

I can still feel the pain deep inside
When I relax and close my eyes
So, I stay on guard and push myself ahead
Because really it would be easy to just cry.

I take control for others to feel better
It helps me to not worry inside
When I am busy no one can see my pain
And I can be happy, and my feelings hide.

I guess it is always going to be with me
I don't have to feel my internal pain
The little girl with the tears in her eyes
Can fade deeper inside with no name.

KAL 18/03/05

I have many memories of just not knowing if I could muster enough energy to get through a day. The only time I seemed to have any charge over myself was when I took on too much and immersed myself into working. If I worked hard and helped others, then I did not have to think about anything or get lost in thought. I became exhausted in life. I kept trying to do more, be more, have more, want more, see more…. just as long as I didn't have to think about me.

I am sure if I had not had the parents and family, I had I would have been more of a statistic then survivor. I should have died many times with activities I embarked on. I know I prayed for death on more than one occasion. I always felt I would have died before I was sixteen. Maybe I really did and somehow carried on. That would explain a lot.

I am here now – why?
I can't figure it out – how?
I should've just died
I don't know what to do now.

I was free and now I'm not
I was supposed to stay home
I didn't and it was a shot.
I'm feeling so all alone.

I don't want to be here anymore
I should be with those I love
I wish I could go through the door
I, then, could thank God above

I know it's not a bad dream
I wish it was one although
I see the world is not what it seems
I know I've a long, long way to go.

KAL 17/04/23

My rants and raving here do help me start to put my life and tribulations into neat little slots. Pulling my thoughts out of that small little girl is giving way to a more understanding of where my life has come from. I pray over and over it also will steer a clear path to leaving this world. I, also, pray I can give that little girl a stairway to Heaven herself. Maybe with me, maybe before me. I hope before so she can tell my loved ones there what happened and that I do not hold any of them responsible for it. I figure I did good as I did not become a drug addict or alcoholic. I lived; I suppressed the darkness within my nights so that I could manage through each day. I felt alive when I could help someone else.

My world spins around
And inside it I must stay.
My life falls behind
And my head down I do lay.
Now and then I find
I am losing my firm grasp.
And I must then try
My love not to let lapse.

I have tried real hard
To keep up my side of life.
I have even gave in
To some toil and some strife.
When I think about all
The paths I have been on,
Some have been so short
Yet others have been too long.

My thoughts are muddled
Though I am coping with them.
My insights grow dim
But I take life on the chin.
If I seem distant,
It's only because I am.
I will continue until
Life I will then let win.

My eyes are open
And I see light shining in.
My problems are small
I will conquer, I will win.
Don't think I'll crack
I'm not finished inside.
I will have my love
And my God in which to confide.

TOBY

CAMP CUPCAKE

God help me but I sit here and can feel words trying to take over what I am writing. She wants so badly to be free. She wants to be released and get out of my thoughts and my nights. How can I write fast enough to give her that? I can put thoughts into poetry and such from her and from others close to me.

I might as well embark a little on my stint away from home. The elephant in the room or should I say my life…. In prison, I met some pretty scary women. Scary and afraid of themselves. They had back stories that they shared with me. I left knowing I was there for not only myself or Toby, but I was there for them. Those I connected with needed someone to just listen without judgement and to give them permission to free themselves from their demons. Mind you I do not think of Toby as a demon. She just has demons attached to her thoughts. This was for me as well as for a few of the women I met.

My first night was in lock up in our city. A blanket that was starched beyond useable. And no mattress, just a cement block to lay on.

Transportation from Cranbrook to Oliver was let us say interesting. It was March and I had no sweater, just a short shirt and dress pants. It was not heated in the van. They stopped in Nelson and picked up a crazy, crazy woman. She was out of her cuffs in minutes. She was an eerie woman. Once we got to Oliver, we were put into a big holding cell together and left there for hours. She climbed the walls, literally she did. They came in twice to get her off the top of the wall separating the toilet and benches. They threatened her a few times. Once on our way to the 'warehouse' she told me to watch how fast she gets out of there.

We got to the spot they keep the women and she immediately flitted from table to table talking to all the women. I, on the other hand, just wanted to know where they wanted me. Thankfully, they put me up top and, in the corner, away from the crazy lady. Although they forgot me a couple times at mealtime. They said they were not used to having anyone in that cell. It was a small two bunk room with a toilet and sink. The little mattress did nothing for sleep and I was not being given my medications, so I was in dire pain. I asked and the guards said they would investigate into it. Six days later when I left for Maple Ridge Alouette Correctional Centre for Women, known better as Camp Cupcake, I finally got my meds. But going to a new place meant I would not be getting all of them again. I would stand in line with all the woman waiting for their 'Prescribed drugs' instead of their street drugs. They kept them stoned instead of helping them dry out and break free of it all. That burned my butt because some of those girls just would say they had a drug problem to get the high. Others wanted to break free but did not know how. I will circle back later.

That crazy lady back in Oliver did manage to get sent to the psych ward at the hospital as she chose to run around naked and yell obscenities. I passed by her cell once and she whispered, 'this is how you do crazy'.

My voice is strong, yet no one hears
I try to explain, through my dry tears

My voice is mine, but it goes unheard
I want to say it, and they hear no words

My voice is true, although they say lies
I've tried to help them, and I only sigh

My voice is soft, and now quieter I get
I slowly give up, no one has heard me yet

My voice has gone silent, they don't ever see
I am gone, no longer am I me....

KAL 17/05/15

I wrote with fervor once again. Words came flying out of my mind onto paper. I could not have enough time to write. My empathic side heard others in the night. I would awaken and write. I would feel their pain. I would once again help others so that I might help myself.

Fears are all around
  Can you feel them?
Worry is on my mind
  Will it stop or when?

Pain creeps up again
  How can you cope?
Thoughts make you sad
  Won't you lose hope?

Love seems all gone
  Why am I crying?
Desolation takes over
  Where will I be dying?

Time is short for you
  What does it matter?
Hope dwindles away
  Is it now or later?

KAL 17/04/28

The six months I was there did not fly by fast enough. They crushed my meds and made most of them ineffective. There were two of the nurses that did not crush them and that was well appreciated. Can you imagine standing in a line up, walking up to a window, opening your mouth so the guard can look in it, getting your meds in a small cup, dumping them into your mouth, taking a drink of water and them opening your mouth for the guard again? I understand the concept but there should be a better way so that you can get the proper meds in the way they were intended. I had two that were in capsule form and needed to be slow release. We were only allowed to get our meds at a certain time in the morning and again at night. My night meds were worn off by the time I tried to go to sleep. I guess I should just be happy that I got them.

My first night in maximum this is what came to me in the middle of the night. My roommate came with me and about four others from Oliver to Maple Ridge. She seemed lost and she seemed so sad. Tough but sad. I was glad to be with her. I felt safer with her around. In the morning when I read this to her. She slumped down the wall with tears in her eyes and looked at me and said, "wow, that is me. How did you know this is how I feel?" She decided she liked me, and I was safe there. My empathic soul was in tune with her.

I can't hear you any more
   As I slide down to the floor.
The buzzing is in my head
   As I look at the blood so red.
I know you are standing there
   But my eyes just can't see where
I feel yet another blow
   You know that is all I know.
You will soon have to stop and leave
   And I will clean up and grieve.
I hear the door as it slams shut
   I know I'll never get out of this rut.
As I clear around me yet again,
   The tears start to fall like a slow rain.
Soon you will return again to me
   Making me believe it's my fault really.
Others say I should pack up and go
   They don't understand this is all I know.
To try and break this chain; start a new life
   Would you come find me and cause me strife?
If I did try to leave you and run
   I'd be dead in the street by knife or by gun.
So, I close my eyes and hang my head low
   The tears come fast and give up I know
When will it be over and when will I heal?
   I'm not brave; I'm weak; I no longer feel.

KAL 17/04/10

It was here that I met an interesting soul. Johnny – she was the main person you want on your side on the inside. She ate with me and after the first meal, she said, "okay, tell me why you are here because you don't look like you should be." I agreed and said my thoughts exactly. So, I asked her if she had ever watched 'Fried Green Tomatoes'. She did not remember if she had. I said when you do watch the parking lot scene. I laughed and said, "the bitch took my parking spot, what else could I do?" She laughed and said she liked me and to not tell anyone why except what I just told her. She said I will tell everyone you are a bad ass, and they will leave you alone.

Going out into medium security was day and night. Here were fifty or so women from all walks of life hanging out like church camp. We had assigned rooms with doors that we locked. We could use a regular bathroom with doors so no one can see you do your business. You can take a shower again with a door for privacy. You eat in a mess hall but hey we are at church camp right! More a little later about this interesting turn of events in my life.

Feeling down and blue
    Don't know what to do
Can't seem to just think
    Thinking life just stinks

Not sure where to turn
    Or know if I'll ever learn
Can't trust that anyone cares
    Life is only cruel and unfair

Want to just lay down now
    Don't care about tomorrow
My body wants to give in
    Would dying be a sin?

Can't believe in anyone
    My mind is all but done
Needing something to believe
    Would anyone notice or grieve

KAL 17/04/25

So many emotions I had bottled up, but you know I did not hear my small voice as often because of all the noise in my head from the others. There were so many stories and lives in turmoil around me, besides my own shadow.

I met some interesting women. Many much like me and we became close friends to keep our own sanity. The guards became friends with us also as they said they had never had so many normal women around. We joked, we talked, and we walked a lot. Roommates came and went. We moved from building to building and back again a couple times. A baby was born and whisked away. I learnt what the effects of drugs and alcohol does to a person's mind. Many were not much pass acting like teenagers. It is true that when a person becomes addicted, they do not mature past the age they were at when they started. One of the sad things about jail is you dumb yourself down to cope with the others. I saw that and felt that. I would have to pull myself away from that drama and remind myself I was not here for a long time nor a good time.

I could feel their loneliness within themselves. I acknowledged how they felt and many I just tried to listen to how they felt. How they acted did not match their own spirits within. Most were Indigenous Canadians. There were twelve of us mature (over fifty) and a couple just over thirty that formed an alliance to keep ourselves from dumbing down. It is true that when you are housed with addicts you find yourself slipping down to their level of intelligence. I met addicts, hookers, high priced call girls, thieves of all kinds, sad young women that were coerced by older, manipulative people, mature women that should not have been there, including myself. It was scary. It was hard. It was unnecessary. There was four women over sixty-five. One had horrible diabetes. One wanted to end her life. One had no idea why she was there as she had dementia. And one was in a wheelchair and had severe medical issues. I had to pick her up as she had fallen out of her bed. I had to break out of the front door and run to the gym where methadone and suboxone was given to the women and yell at a guard to get our emergency exit unlocked so I could wheel her to medical as I could not carry her down the steps. I will talk about the fact that they do not dry addicts out. They keep them high but on 'legal' drugs. And when they get out, they get it free with a prescription. Sad yes.

The justice system is broken. People were being subjected to a lifestyle that did not match their crime. We were told that there were about eighteen of us that should have been in the empty homes just outside the perimeters under minimum security with the choice to get a job and move about freely within Maple Ridge. Why were we not there? We heard many excuses. Not enough funds, not enough guards, not enough room, not enough interest, not enough women. We were allowed to clean the two houses so they could show off the places to the community watchdogs wondering why they help funded the building of the minimum houses. They had many excuses, but they could not pinpoint the exact reason. I swore I was going to raise the roof and write all about this and I will return to this thought wave. I will say my own problems seemed trivial compared to the trials and tribulations of those I met.

Being there helped was a start to want to heal. I will swing back to my time there a little later. There is so much to talk about. Someone has to get the story out that this is not the place for most of the women that are there, were there, will be there.

Hurt and Crying
   Pain now Sighing
      Nothingness to me
         Dark and Gloomy
            Unloved and Denied
               Afraid and Defied
                  Depressed and Cold
                     Feeling so Old
                     Secure so Stronger
                  Healing now Longer
               Independent and Fine
            All is well in time
         Controlled and Happy
      Pleased to be me
   Soon to be Free
Learning to love me

KAL 17/04/24

I must visit my time at Camp Cupcake in Maple Ridge as it was an important discovery time for me. I was overwhelmed with the thoughts and pains of everyone I came in contact, and I wrote like a demon. They were not all my thoughts. They were being communicated to me through their dreams and a few from talking together. It is sad that more than five of the souls I felt are no longer with us. I lift their souls to God praying He is holding them safe and sound finally.

Screams, pain, fear
    Sweat, foul smell in the air
Blackout, bruises, cuts
    Broken bones don't care.

Crawling, gasping, struggle
    Dirty, hungry too.
Fading, sleepy, tired
    All life is through.

KAL 17/04/19

This is about a beautiful young woman I met in medium security. She did not speak to many, but she had a wonderful soul inside. She was lost and now she is gone. Her demons took her all too soon. She was just starting to live. Her father's death had spiralled her down into the dark drug world. While at Camp Cupcake she turned her life around and was accepted to a program. I know she was doing well, but her previous life came back and claimed her again. I was terribly upset to hear of her passing. The potential she had was outstanding.

She looks out the window and sees the rain
Then looks at her arm and watches her vein
It looks like she soon will not feel any pain
She hangs her head and has no more shame
As she stumbles along; falls onto her bed
Her body starts to shake, and her arm turns red
They all know about what she is and heard what was said
Soon it won't matter when she is found dead
Her eyes flutter open and she sees her loving dad
He's been gone ten years but was the best she had
The day he had died she was so upset and sad
And after he'd been buried, she walked around mad
He told her it wasn't her time; she had   to live today
She held on tightly and asked him, please daddy stay
But she looked around and, in a hospital, she now lay
She watched as the doctors said she'd be okay
It's been a hard time trying to not do the same things
But she walks with her head up and doesn't do bad things

No more drugs, no more lies; just clean living as she sings
Tomorrow she will be clean and sober, no more part of a drug ring

KAL 17/04/24

Amanda was one of my room mates and we had fun together. We laughed often when laying in our bunks about life. She had an infectious laugh. Her family was strong, but her heart was weak. She believed when a man said they would treat her right and take care of her, he would. She left her family and travelled across Canada to start a fresh life with one of the men she thought she loved. Not even a month later she no longer laughs, loves, or breathes. She is gone. Such potential to do good and a family that loved her did not keep her safe from that one man that promised the moon yet took her life away.

She looks up at the moon
As she fights back her tears
She wonders who she is now
And if anyone still cares
It wasn't that long ago
She thought she had it all
Somewhere along her path
Is when she did fall
   Although she has struggled
   She pushed to gain back her life
   But she only feels good
   When she sees the blade of a knife
   Her tears fall silently now
   And she is all but gone
   The pain, the strife and loneliness
   Will be over soon, not long.
She can still see the moon
Shining down upon her face
But soon her thoughts will leave.
Her mind will leave this space
The night slips slowly away
And the moon is now blood red
She will rest her weary soul.
The pain is gone; she is dead!

KAL 17/09/08

I still cry when I think of Amanda. I can still see her smiling face. It is hard to say goodbye to someone that did not know you were praying they made the right choice to move. She must have known I would question if it was a good thing to leave her kids with her family and go with this man that she did not know as well. But she was in love again. Amanda trusted it would work out. I miss you Amanda and I hope you are laughing in Heaven.

She stands in the rain as the tears fall from her eyes
She knew it wasn't right to believe in all his lies
She didn't want to think that the truth had hurt her so
She would have to face them all and now they all would know

He didn't think it would have hurt but her tears were real
He wasn't thinking when into the night, love he did steal
He just got caught up and soon it was too late
He knew now it meant the end and this was his fate

They tried so hard to keep up the charade and make others think
They still loved each other although they were no longer a link
They now would go their separate ways into the looming dark
They wouldn't have each other and new lives they would start

Why can't life be easier and why is she hurting so?
Why now is she still crying; why now she doesn't know?
When will she realize that she is strong enough to leave?
When will she learn to trust and who to believe?

KAL 17/04/28

I cannot talk about Camp Cupcake without talking about Angel. This girl was definitely something. She had a hard life. Her first-time selling dope was when she found her stepdad's stash and went down to the corner store and sold it. She was five and her life was set there and then. She sold drugs, she took drugs, she kidnapped a man that owed her money and landed herself at Camp Cupcake. She tried hard to now return to the life but became overwhelmed once she was out and had an unpleasant experience with a man. She is trying hard right now to get out of the game again and I pray that happens for her. She really is a beautiful soul and I miss her sunny smile. I worry for her life, and I worry that I will lose her too soon also. Angel if you are out there, you are loved and deserve to be happy and safe always.

She struggles with her life as she gazes at the moon
She doesn't know if all the pain will be over soon
Looking back, she should have known life could be so mean
If she can get through it all still had to be seen.

What can she do to make life change for her now?
Will there be anyone lift to help and show her how?
She looks around and wonders how it got this bad
All the mistakes and failures now make her sad.

Why didn't she stay true to all she had been taught?
If she had listened to others, it would have changed a lot?
Shrinking against the wall the tears start to fall.
Maybe it is time to just go ahead and end it all.

As the night ends and turns into another day
It is quiet all around her, she won't see today.
Bright red engulfs her body as she lay on the floor
No more worries, no more guilt as there is nobody anymore.

KAL 17/07/21

My heart breaks when I think of Layla. Man, that girl had a voice and when we would have Sunday evening church, she could belt every song aloud and clear. I could sit and listen to her for hours. She really was a lost little girl. She told me about her childhood and all the hard knocks she was dealt. Even with all the trauma she believed in God and her faith was so strong. She wanted a better life. Layla stayed in touch with me after she was released, even up until her sudden death. She messaged me for strength and to pray for her. That was the day she was found dead. It was not something she did to herself, she was killed I know it. I left a message for her family that I had information they may want regarding Layla's last evening. They never have but she knew she was in danger and that whatever it was she was doing that evening may be her last breath on earth. My heart hurt so much when I found out that she was no longer with us. I hope my sister and my parents are watching over her in Heaven.

Remembering Layla and her infectious smile reminds me how quickly life can change. She was leaving Camp Cupcake to go live with one of her church's families. She was so excited to start fresh and keep away from the life she knew. I was so proud to have the opportunity to get to know her. She was like Tigger and bounced everywhere. She tried so hard to get to know others. Many shunned her as crazy. Most endured her. I loved her energy and how open she was about everything. She was going to better her life and sing in the church choir. How fragile is life?

Tears fall silently;
 Memories wiped clear.
 All that ever was
 Or even held so dear.
 What God had given
 Slips through my hand
 The devil steps inside
 Now the sins of man
 Quietly we give in
 Know what has been done
 There's no turning back
 Once you've hurt the one
 Secretly it all happens
 And with that God above
 Takes it all away
 Even takes those you love

KAL 17/05/31

Some nights at Camp Cupcake were lonely. I had a few nights by myself in between roommates and those nights were long. My fibro pain was on high alert and my foggy brain had trouble comprehending my total existence. I am so glad there were not many of those nights by myself. I had bad nights even with roomies but at least I had someone to talk to before rolling over on my cot and wishing I were somewhere else. My legs ached, my head ached, my body ached, and my heart ached. It was the worst six months of my life.

Voices are heard all around me, yet no others in the room I see.
My body shouts out in spastic pain, I've tried every position where I've lain.
Again, I look about my life, the pain feels worse than the knife.
I toss, I turn, I feel the bitter cold, life is fragile; will I grow old?
My heart beats sadly in my chest, I don't know who I am or what is left.
Others look like they too feel what I feel; is it a fantasy or is this real?
Nights are long and such a sad time, loneliness, emptiness, a stupid crime.
Wishing for my family is always on my mind, but can you see them, just that'd be fine.

I can't believe how lonely a heart can be, and how your head buzzes like a bee.
When you can't live life as you think. And no longer are in control – gone in a wink!

KAL 17/04/09

I cannot get a lot of vision of dreams I had while there out of my thoughts now. And knowing so many have passed on since just 5 years ago. The following passages were so vivid and left me so tired and sad. Most of these girls just needed a chance or a change.

The gun is loaded; pointed to her head
Just one pull and down she falls dead.

The needle is spent and falls to the floor
She'll never feel pain anywhere anymore.

She hides behind the door locked tight
Why, oh why, is everything about the fight.

Cringing she crawls thru the broken glass
Her blood leaves her body way too fast.

The warmth of the liquid spreads to her heart
Soon she'll forget today, tomorrow doesn't start.

They were all right; yes, they all told her so
"You'll not be much or amount to anything you know!"

As another punch hits her head again
If she could just die, then there'd be no pain.

What if she hadn't said yes that very first time?
Would she still be caught up in the crime?

KAL 17/04/07

Being with empathetic energy my stay at Maple Ridge (Camp Cupcake) I found myself in conversations with God numerous times.

The system has a group of Christians that came in to talk to anyone who wished to have a visitor. Since I had all these feelings, I readily accepted to have a visitor. The mature lady I placed up with was so pleasant and a wonderful listener. I let her read some of my poetry as it was a way to say how I felt without the words coming directly from me. As she would read, she would get tears in her eyes and bless me. That was very comforting. I enjoyed our twice-monthly visits and was eager for her visit. God was gracious enough to give me this woman. She helped me stay closer to sane than she realizes, although, I am sure God knew what He was doing. I felt closer to Him and closer to some of the pained souls there. I would pray at night for their souls to be blessed and ask God to forgive them for their indiscretions. I was not able to let her know that I was leaving abruptly as I was granted early parole on a Friday and was on a bus the next Monday, I was elated, yet scared, yet sad, yet at peace. It is a funny feeling. The one thing I must stress is they drop you off at the bus station or whatever method they can secure, and you must follow your instincts from there.

What is it Lord that you need from me?
    I've tried everything to prove myself to you.
Is there something I'm missing in Your message?
    Was it anything I should or should not do?

Yesterday I turned the other cheek for you
    When someone said mean things to me.
Today again You challenge me to be quiet
    I'm trying Lord, oh yes, I am, can't you see?

Tomorrow will bring a new day I know
    Though I am faltering and need some guidance.
It's hard to look the other way all the time
    Lord, please help me, give me a chance.

Show me how to be a better person
    And help me to keep my faith strong.
I know I can do Your calling Lord
    So, I can remember to teach right from wrong.

KAL 17/05/21

Regardless of how I felt I know I was still lost. I knew that God has forgiven me but had my family. How were they going to see me now? My innocence was taken from me. I paid a price to protect others and that is who I am. The same people no longer were there for me. I had to stop in Kamloops for almost two weeks before I could go home. John and Krychelle came to get me as I was free to go at midnight on the 29th of September. It was a long time for me. I counted the days in and the days to get home. Too many nights away from the ones I loved. I have never told any of them that I feel the difference in them since. The young grandchildren were the ones that gave me the same love from before. Oh, how I prayed for God to watch over them while I was not there to do it myself. It has been a few years and I still get a little panicked when I see the courthouse, the sheriff's van, and the cop shop. I wake up thinking I am back there in medium security and a flashlight is shining into the room to make sure we are in bed. Advise to the weary, do not protect others that do not deserve it. You pay the price dearly and forever.

What is wrong? What do I mean?
What can I say? What is now seen?
Questions I have. Answers I've not
I've looked everywhere. Nothing is sought!

Can this be true? Can I still exist?
Can I understand? Can I get what is missed?
I turn around, I try to make sense.
I want more for me. I have no defence!

Will I make it back? To where I once had been?
Will I be the same? Will a change be seen?
More questions I have. Still lingering inside
I ask to God above. As I in Him confide!

When will I be whole? When is the time?
When can I relax? When will I see the sign?
I look to You each hour. To help me find my way
I trust in Your love. To bring me home one day!

KAL 17/07/01

I let God into my soul there. I have always been a Christian and felt God's love within my heart. Being in the depths of evil at Camp Cupcake allowed me to just be. Just let God give me direction. Since I have been back home it has been hard to know where to go to be closer to God. I have tried a few churches and I have decided that God is closest to me right at home. Out back in the middle of nature I can hear the song of the angels come through the trees. I felt that when I would just sit in a gazebo and let the breeze talk to me. It was relaxing.

When everything seems wrong
There is still more to do
It will be all made right
Take a breath and think anew

Don't let anguish in your soul
Take over your mind and cry
Hold onto the positive
Breathe deep, eyes open sigh.

Where we are now is not
Where we will be for life
It will all be over soon
No more tears, pain or strife

We get each other through
Each day and the long nights
Be brave, smile, look forward
Happiness and home are in sight.

KAL 17/09/10

Many of the girls there did self harm a lot to ease the pain of the life they were leading. There were prostitutes, a bat-shit crazy lady, a madam, a few high-end call girls, drug dealers, fraudsters, shop lifters, mail fraud/theft, an immigration fraud, alcoholic repeater, DUI, and even a 75-year-old woman that was there because her grandson left his stash in her car and never owned up to it. It was crazy. But the nights were hard on me. As an empath, myself, I could feel them tortured in the night. And most days I would spend writing down their nightmares.

The razor is sharp and slices down my arm
    Each vein, each tendon wide open with pain.
The droplets start and then flow freely now
    A puddle forms on the ground like rain.

I can't control who I was or look in your eyes
    I know I hurt you so I'm giving you your space.
You will always be deep within my soul
    I'll just be another DOA in some detective's case.

The world was mine and I threw it all away
    We could have had it all, but the party was on.
All the lights, the fights, the speed, the drugs and the booze
    Caught up with me and I don't want another sun.

We always knew it would happen almost this way
    Whether a knife, a bullet, a needle or a crash.
I chose to end it with a blade held in my hand
    And the blood draining out of my arm fast.

So, as I drift asleep, and my head feels heavy
    I think of you and know you will be alright.
My thoughts no longer make sense to me
    And I'll fall down and say goodbye into the night.

KAL 17/04/15

My stay there comes back once in awhile and I have a nightmare I would have there. They are very real, and it makes it hard to get a good night's sleep. A counsellor I had just after I got home said there may be residual PTSD because living for 6 months away from my loved ones without seeing them and being amid the turmoil that is correctional prisons can linger. I pray every night for the young girls and the women I met. I cry when I hear one of them has passed or returned to their old life. I will say the system does not help them at all. They keep them high on suboxone or methadone so when they leave, they have free prescriptions to maintain them. They will return to illegal drugs once those run out. Why not dry them out while they are there? After a few bad withdrawal nights, they would be done and over while there and stay that way. Who knows, it is worth a try. The stupid meaningless programs they have are aimed at young teenagers. Well, some of those girls never got past being thirteen or so, but if you dumb down everything, the people around dumb down. There were a few of us that had to dumb down to have a conversation with most of the others. It is a broken system.

The things I see within this world
Are not simple or sweet anymore
I used to see the beauty in a rose bud
But now I see thorns and close my door

Once I use to look into the blue sky
And dream of places I would visit one day
But the dark clouds have replaced my horizon
So now I feel captured and here I will stay

If ever I could change how things now are
I would paint a new and different scene
I'd see bluer skies and all my budding roses
My doors would open and again I would dream

I need the simple and sweet in life now
I could walk freely and look for my peace
Just to be myself and feel love again
To feel better and make all pain decrease

But, alas, I look around this place once more
And I don't see what it is that I need
The world is harsh, cold and disturbed; not mine
I will wait for a change; I will plant a seed.

KAL 17/08/20

I have never said anything about steps I could have taken to keep myself out of jail. I did not throw anyone under the bus, nor did I give names of those that could have backed up what happened. The funny thing is the ones that I protected were the most vocal and disrespectful to me. I forgive them as they really do not know where they could have ended up also. The most amusing thing was the boss tried to get the judge to throw an extra $200,000 from me to him. The numbers were never that high as no one allowed my lawyer or myself to critique the audit. I must repay $15,000 and that is even more then I owed. My boss put a claim into his insurance for almost $300.000 and they paid him minus $15,000. He recouped a profit of $280,000, sold his business here and bought a bigger one in Ontario. This man defrauded the courts, defrauded his insurance company and the employees of the store he left behind. Those fellow workers did not know that he had done this to them. He convinced them that I must have taken the money from profit sharing. The judge asked him why he did not share the insurance money with the employees. His answer was that his lawyer and accountant said he did not have to. Wow and I am the felon????!!! I should not say all of them did not know, as a couple reached out to me to ask the questions that told them how he ran off with their monies also. Funny how rich people work. Karma comes to those who do not own up to their mistakes or make right the wrong they caused to so many.

Have you ever thought you knew it?
Then find out you weren't even close.
And when you tried to figure it out
You were wrong again; you didn't know

Have you tried to be available for others?
Only to have them turn their backs on you.
And no matter what you wanted to say
There was nothing you could change or do.

Is it possible that you should turn away?
And make yourself start not to care?
It seems that if you try too long and hard
You start to feel sad and that is not fair.

Will it ever make a difference to anyone?
If you do keep trying or if you just give up?

You will have to make that decision yourself
But know it may never be enough!

KAL 17/08/24

As I have said I talked to a lot of guards and residents at the hoosgow. I love that word. The guards talked to me a lot and told me stories. The repeat offenders they see year in, year out. As I saw them come back it made sense. This place was their three meals a day and a roof over your head. Or as they said three squares and a squat. Remarkably interesting stories and the difference in stories from time to time makes one laugh. They are so drug induced they forget the story they used last time. You do what you are told, and you get along with everyone so that you can leave sooner than later. The doors are locked most of the time and you must ask permission if you need to go to the 'big house', that is maximum. Now there you are nothing. You have no identity except your last name, and you must watch others the few hours you are allowed to step out of your hole, I mean room. Outside consist of a small courtyard that is covered with a metal slat roof. You line up for your meals. You sit at a small metal table. Everything is metal. You do have a mattress that is about three" thick and prickly blankets with one pillow. The other mantra most these girls will say 'straight at the gate, gay for the stay.' I actually watched one older straight woman take on an interest in one of the repeat offenders and start a blooming relationship that carried outside of their release and was good until the younger one fell back into her old ways and went back to Maple Ridge. Such a different life there. Or should I say no life there.

I used to be the one in control of my own life
I was mother, sister, daughter, friend, and wife
Now as I try to understand where I am
It is so hard to think and do what I can
> It is surreal time, and I don't know what to do
> But I'm trying hard to look up and try something new
> Others are the ones that now make decisions for me
> I can hardly wait for the day I will be free

Lessons learned by many I hear all the stories
From all walks of life, they come and talk to me
They've done many things that they are so sorry for
They are trying so hard and out of life want more

Some are here, I find, too many times again
They don't know how to break free of their own chains
I know I won't see most ever again after this
As I won't falter, but they may slide back to their abyss

I need to be free again and take care of myself
Hang up my problems and place them on a shelf
The days are long for all of us, as well as the weeks
Someday, somehow, we all find the power we seek.
God help us!

KAL 17/05/25

These women had a passion for something, but no support to cultivate it. I could see the sparkle in their eyes when they spoke. Wanda could knit like nobody's business and had such love for animals. She lived in a tent squatting on property with a multitude of others without homes. Wanda had a house at one time and her dogs were her life. Soon she found that property owners were not okay with pets, and she moved into tent city. She worked in the lumber mill attached to the prison. The owner looked at her as a supervisor. I know she could function in the world. Instead, she chose to live on the wrong side of the tracks. The deaths she has seen from overdose and destruction would curl anyone's hair.

You just feel at a loss of how to help these people. I stay in touch and thankfully she is not one of the lost lives due to drugs or violence. This woman was a drug dealer, only to survive. She was so careful to maintain safe drugs, yet some fentanyl made it into some, and she was immediately picked up and charge. I often wonder if she was not set up by another dealer to take over her area. I do not condone drug use or dealing, but I do understand why some are hell bent on doing so. Marsha was a hoot. We were close to the same age, and both enjoyed a wry sense of humour. We shared that and were there almost for the same reason. I loved that she was someone with whom I could talk.

We played euchre together and tried to teach others. We had a charades evening and that was so funny. We all laughed so hard. It was great to see others relaxing and enjoying a simple life. I just wished that they did not return to their old lives when they left. Sadly, many did.

Marsha and I decided to tell some of the ladies that came a mixture of the story of our ill-fated life that brought us to Alouette. I carried on with the story Johnny told me to talk about the parking space with grandeur and jest. Marsha would tell a story of a crazy church lady that smashed into the back of her car over and over. She would say that all would have been okay except the trunk of her car popped opened as the police came and well where else would you put a dead body?! It took a few ladies to sit back and think about it then you would see a light come on and link our stories. It was a gas to just have a little innocent fun.

This may not be the life I've dreamt
But it is the reality I will face.
I never meant to be travelling this road
But the reason God put it here is the case.

I know He has chosen this path for me
And I will look deep and be His servant.
Others elate themselves as I will march on
And those in faith and love will see the want.

Forgiveness has been asked from God above
For myself, for others especially the ones in need.
I can't let their negative thoughts inside
Because all hate needs is a little seed.

I will go where needed and I will trudge on
I will face each day with the love God gave me.
The tears I shed are not for me, but those I love
And who needs God's love to live and be free.

Please don't worry or cast doubts over others
Smile and love and be patient with one another.
Know God has a purpose for all of us
Same, but different; always for each other.

KAL 17/04/08

Kristi was my last room mate, and she was a welcomed relief. We both worked in laundry and took care of the guard's dogs. It was fun to have someone that you could carry on a conversation with. I will say she whipped me into shape. We walked, we talked, we read in the gazebo, we just clicked. I love that we are still in contact, and she lives close enough we could get together if we find the time. We connected and I felt like a mom again. I love her for bringing back some normality to my stay.

Kristi also kept me going to get back in shape. We walked ten miles one day on the path, just to prove it could be done. I could do ten reps of sit ups by the time I left. That is 100 sit ups. I had never in my life been able to do five, so I was impressed with myself and thankful for a great coach.

> A smile is just a smile
> Unless it's given to you.
> A hug is just a hug
> Until it's only for you.
> A tear is just a tear
> Unless it's shed for you.
> A friend is just a friend
> Until they are there for you.

TOBY 05/14/95

There is so much more I want to talk about. Alouette may be better than Oliver, but with a broken justice system it is not serving those that are sentenced well. The guards can only do so much, and I commend their efforts to do what they do. An overhaul from above must happen. The judges doing the sentencing should visit where the inmates go and the system itself needs to do change to adapt to the needs of the inmates. Not easier, do not get me wrong. I mean challenge these ladies to do better. Give them life skills that are meaningful. Show them how to get away from their *damned* lives. Give them the courage to leave the drugs, the alcohol, the homelessness behind and become a productive member of society. The confidence to be someone. It cannot be done the way it is right now. The community watchdog group should visit more often and get things rolling for minimum security and put those that should be there into the home.

BACK TO FREE LIFE

Going back to my inner voice, my crutch, my soul, my little girl. I wrote poetry and songs (much like my gramps) to escape from reality to an extent. It gave me a release as well as the shadows shrunk a little when I immersed myself into writing. In high school I put some of my poetry into a small booklet and put it together as one of my assignments in Business & Communications. I ran off a dozen or so copies and gave them to my grandparents and other family members. When my gramps' sister passed years later her son gave it to my mom to give back. He said his mom liked to read them from time to time. She felt like she was reliving some of her childhood he said. So maybe I had a connection to her thoughts.

My gramps told me a few stories once I grew up that made more sense to me. There was the one where his sister's husband had passed, and she took her daughter and son to live in Saskatchewan. Within the year she had married and at in her forties had had another son. Her teenage daughter was getting married to her new husband's brother. So, mother and daughter would become sisters. He told me that sometimes people move to protect the integrity of the ones they love. That made sense too when he said her son was not only her daughter's brother, but he was his sister's son. Phew that took a while to process. I laugh now and say the roots to some trees intermingle and twist around each other much like family trees. To add to the story. Our great aunt's granddaughter who would be my second cousin is now married to my brother. Those roots get more and more interesting as you watch the tree grow. And her sister married her deceased husband's brother. Just found that out years later.

Why this shone on me was I wondered about my own family tree. Does it come from the same root as my siblings? Does it twist around a bit? I just do not know. My mom always said our root was strong, straight, and solid, so I will take her word for it.

We all have stories within our lives that make life interesting. Some are filled with happiness and love, some with hatred and fear. I have seen the happiness. I have seen the love. I have seen the hatred. I have seen the fear. I also have seen so much more. With happiness there is freedom, yet we will experience constraint within. With love you get excitement, warmth, but also confusion. With hatred you have pain and anger, but also clarity. With fear you can feel the adrenaline, yet we feel close to death.

I had a cousin, Darlene, who had Down's Syndrome. Her great uncles on her mom's side also were this way. I loved her and we had many great times on the farm together. Her younger sister was a spoiled brat who I could not stand. Her older brother was on the borderline of being like her and her older sister was the nicest person around. Her mom was a twig with a cigarette hanging out of her mouth and her dad scared me to death. Her baby sister would torment her, and I defended her all the time. I even got a spanking at the hands of her dad because she whined to him that Darlene was getting special treatment, and I would not let her sleep in my spare bed. I had made a bed for her on the floor. Isn't that where trash goes? I know, not nice but she was a vile human being. Darlene was afraid of many things, and one was corn silk. She would go into the fields and get some for the cornfield and start tormenting her until I would hear it and take it from her. She would run to her daddy and tell him I hurt her, and I would be in trouble again. But I would not allow her to do anything mean to Darlene when I was around. They came often in the summertime. Darlene would come many times by herself to stay and I loved her. I was going on nine one year and she was 14 or 15. She asked me about the birds and the bees. I told her what I knew and then told my sisters that they should talk to her because I was not the person to ask. They tried to put her mind at ease. I think she was worried that she was going to get pregnant because her brother was molesting her. I told her she should tell her parents, but she was afraid to say anything. I know how she felt, and we were close. I did tell her to scream next time. I had not taken control of my own hell yet, but I told her to do what I would do. Her brother left home shortly after so maybe she did. Once her older sister married and had kids, she had Darlene come live with her and help with the babies. She was so proud to be useful.

Darlene was sure she was pregnant from about twenty to this day with Charlie Pride's child. She loved listening to his records. She would spend hours listening over and over. She was happy and did not hurt a fly with her thoughts, so no one challenged her. I miss being young when Darlene was around. She gave me purpose.

Darlene never missed a beat when I would run into her shopping to tell me she was still carrying Charlie's baby.

Her younger sister met Karma in her twenty's unfortunately or maybe fortunately. She had four kids by three different men and had just moved on with another man. Her kids all lived with the father of the two youngest and he raised them. Her then boyfriend and her were killed in a head on crash. Do not get me wrong that is horrible, but it made life for her 4 kids more settled and outright better off.

God bless Darlene being in my life. She helped a sad little girl feel a little different. Love her always. It is true – she is a special angel for those she meets.

Always in a hurry, my life just spins around.
Always looking for some peace that has not yet been found.

Looking all over this world to find my special niche.
Looking for what is right, not knowing which is which.

Running around in circles, it makes me really dizzy.
Running myself down and my life seems so fuzzy.

Trying to do my best to hold my head up high.
Trying to belong to life, but I don't know why.

Feeling very lonely even when I'm not alone.
Feeling very insecure even though I'm now grown.

Hearing nothing while I stand amongst a crowd.
Hearing too much as it grows ever so loud.

Wanting to change my life, but I know not how.
Wanting to be different than I am now.

Needing to believe that someday I will change.
Needing to trust and believe in life without pain.

Seeing myself trying, but not getting anywhere.
Seeing nothing in everything, but I don't care.

TOBY

I do not know why but growing up on a farm with so much going on
and people coming and going you think I would have felt safe. I really
did not. I remember at an incredibly early age tossing and turning to
try and sleep every night and waking up groggy and hating my life.
After the boarder moved on, I found myself saying sexual innuendos.
People laughed and thought nothing of it. My dad told some raunchy
jokes when the adults were sitting around, and I would listen in so
not a big thing. But I was quite brazen because I had a lot of
questions. I had secrets and, in a way, I think I was trying to get
someone to notice me and maybe ask questions.

The only attention I got was unwanted to say the least. I had a cousin
who wanted to have sex with me, and I was evasive. I would hide
whenever he came over to keep him away. Once I started growing
older, I managed that easier with a 'no.' To whom could I talk? My
brother. Right. I did and ended up with him testing out his sexual
desires on me whenever he caught me alone. I had not had my period
yet but one day in January of 1972 I did, and I was so afraid for the
next time he trapped me. I cried for hours worried that I would be
pregnant. My mom thought it was because of having my period. I got
brave and told my brother to find a girlfriend. Thank God he did! I
have never told anyone that story in my life. It feels good to say it,
but it still feels wrong and dirty. I was sure if I told anyone it would
be my fault. I was damaged. I was not pretty. I was just an object that
was used sexually. Who would ever love me unless I had sex with
them?

But I started maturing and I took boys noticing me as a remarkable
thing. I only knew that men want women for sex so far, and I was
hoping I would find one that did not. I was in love with each of them
and thought this might be the one. I even kept a somewhat diary of
who, what and how good. In my mind every boy/man I met would
be the one to marry and love me. I was broken for sure. But until I
got older and realized a person is not valued just because they will
have sex with another person.

My first boyfriend, Steve became my 'on and off' from the age of 14
to 18. To me he was the one and I genuinely believe if we had just
run off and married, we would have stayed together forever. Others
would say no to that. He was my first true love. My first everything.
He taught me how to love with a fervor. Such passion I never felt
until my second marriage. He came back into my life for a brief while

when I realized my first marriage was done. I met my second husband, John, just before I was leaving my first husband, Jay, to go to Steve. John showed me that I was stepping backwards in my life and if I went, I was regressing. I needed to go forward. I had even written John a poem and had planned to give it to him when I left, but God had other plans.

Though I'm very fond of you
And this will be hard to say
I can't be more than a friend
Because I need to find my own way

You make me smile and feel fine
I hope I do the same
We can still find time to be together
But love is not the name.

We can laugh and hug together
And make silly grins
We can love like friends
But more passion with us will never win.

I am not able to give my soul
And that's what you deserve
I can only offer my friendship
No more than that I haven't the nerve.

We spoke of feelings and that was good
You and I think alike
But I do belong deep in my heart
To someone else – I'd give him my life.

I've thought long and hard
And though it may feel wrong
I can't love you no matter what
My heart to another does belong.

You must always be secure
And know what a fine man you are
You deserve the best and more
You will in life go far.

KAL 03/15/96

My teenage life was fast and furious. I did so many dangerous things I should have not made it through. Steve would stop his truck just past a train track and then we would lie on the track listening for a train. Most times at a crossing that did not have a crossing alarm. I wish I could say I would love to live that over but no thank you. Would I make a few different decisions – probably. Marrying Jay and having my four wonderful children would not be one of them. Looking back now I think I would have cut my time with Steve off and taken a different road. But as they say all your decisions lead you to where you are now. John came into my life at a crucial time. If not for him, I believe I would have lost my family and even myself.

God must have known
    I had lost my way
It was just when I met you
    I was full of dismay.

We weren't supposed to happen
    But he had greater plans.
For he knew we needed each other
    You offered and I accepted your hand.

For every pothole we encountered
    You stood strong for me to learn
Without our love I knew
    Your love keeps my heart set to burn.

God must have known
    I had lost my way
It was just when I met you
    I was full of dismay.

Life is better now we are together
    My way is clearer now
You bring light into my dark
    Love, not fear and no woe.

KAL 09/23/08

With each guy I knew I was not the sure confident girl. I was dying for someone to love me enough to want me. Steve toyed with my heart. Jay wanted me but I think it was so he could get out of the life he was in. When I met him, he was living on his sister's couch. He had one pair of jeans, an old coat, a couple of t-shirts, a pair of undies and a couple pair of socks beaten up boots. He was floundering himself and I thrive on helping others. My mother called it the 'poor puppy' syndrome. She said all three of her daughters were raised to take care of everyone and we all picked the puppy down in the sewer up, brushed him off and built him into an adult. Jay asked me to marry him about a month after we met. We married 6 months later and stayed together 17 years. No one was to blame for our disintegration of our marriage. We both fell out of love. We were on automatic for the last few years. I know I was slowly dying inside, and I look back on photos and I looked like an empty shell. There was no spark in my eyes. I imagine he, also, was feeling the same. The only difference was I had to decide as he never ever would. Jay lacked confidence and I was too tired to be the only one working on our life together.

I am feeling so alone now
    And the pain of feeling blue
All because so now I don't
    Just reach out and call for you
I thought I was coping fine
    Then you told me there was no more
So right here I will sit down
    And just stare at the closed door
I guess I knew all along
    That it would all come to an end
But it's hard for me to bear
    So, I cry and my head I bend
There is no one else close to me
    That's just the way it is
No hand to hold onto anymore
    No one to hug or no one to kiss
My heart beats more slowly now
    And the tears fall down like rain
I will go on by myself in life
    And be the one to feel the pain.

KAL 17/04/24

Jay knew about some of my childhood trauma. I had told him about being so young and a border assaulting me. I had told him how angry I was at my dad for not protecting me and that was why we were distant. It was after we were married and I was pregnant with our first born, Jaymee that I realized why I was mad at my dad and that was the time my dad and I had that big blow up on our way back to work. It was not my best behaviour and I hated myself after it happened.

We had gone home for lunch from work. My mom, my dad and I that is. On the way back to work I made a big stink over dad smelling like the barn and smoke. I rolled my window down and stuck my head out. After dad dropped us off at the greenhouse and he went to the field I broke down and cried. I think I cried over what happened in my childhood beside what happened with my dad. Our boss, Paul, came to the greenhouse and upon seeing me so upset drove me home. I fell into the bed and cried. Soon after my dad also came home and came to my room and apologized. I told him how sorry I was but never told him the real reason I was so sorry. That day I wrote my dad a letter telling him what happened. That day I ripped that letter up. That day I wrote another letter telling my dad how much I loved him, and it must be my pregnancy that was making me especially mean. I apologized for my childhood and being disruptive and not listening. I apologized over and over and asked for his forgiveness. He hugged me after reading the letter and said he also was to blame and hoped I would forgive him for not understanding how I felt being pregnant. I forgave my dad for the fight, but I also forgave my dad for what happened that he had no idea about. It was not his fault as he never knew, and I vowed my parents would never know. I did not want them to feel they had failed to protect any of us kids. They were terrific parents. I did not fully appreciate them until I was married and starting my own family.

Am I falling Lord
>Or am I failing You?
I've tried so hard
>And know not what to do.
>>Are you listening Lord
>>>And are You hearing me?
>>I am trying my best
>>>I open my eyes to see.
Can I do this Lord
>Or can You show me how?
I can feel a change
>But I'm slipping now
>>Will it be enough Lord
>>>And will others also, see?
>>I'm trying to prove
>>>So, all can forgive me.
Why do I worry Lord
>About all of these things?
I know You love me
>And are with me through everything.
>>Am I going to be alright Lord
>>>And am I standing tall?
>>I'm trying to keep my smile.
>>>Just waiting for Your call!

KAL 17/07/15

I had released some of my pent-up anger after all that. Now I had to move forward. I buried a lot of the pain and anger that was left. I immersed myself into my little family. Jaymee was born in 1980, Kayla was born in 1983, Joshua was born in 1987 and Krychelle in 1989. I was so happy to have these four beautiful children. I was a hard parent though and for that I am not proud. I could have been more lenient, more trusting, more encouraging, more understanding. My oldest, God love him, got the worse part of my parenting as I was not sure I could do this. My husband was a great parent. He was hands on and there for our children while they were babies.

If I were to think back, he was great up to when they surpassed his comfort zone as he felt he lacked the confidence to help them once they went into high school. Jay did not complete grade 6 let alone the next three grades as he was pushed into each grade and failed to attend. But he was a wonderful father. Whenever we went to family gatherings you would find him outside with the kids. Whether playing with them or just keeping a watchful eye on them. Our kids were incredibly lucky to have him as a dad.

I knew his short comings. I tried to gently push him into believing more in himself, but he had his demons also. Jay was into drugs and drinking when I met him. He did not have a stable family life. All his family were into drinking or drugs or both. I was aware of this when we married. In fact, a few weeks before our wedding I sat him down and told him I was not going through with a marriage if he was going to continue the same road he was on. I did not make him quit drugs and drinking. I just openly told him that if he wanted me and to get married, he had to leave behind all that. If he wanted to do keep up with the drugs and drinking, then I was moving on. Love him or not I was not adding that conflict to my already painful life.

I let Jay make his own mind up and I patiently waited the next day for his decision. We met up and had a great talk. He did not want to end up like his parents. He wanted a different path in his life, and he needed me to help him through. I loved him with most of my heart. As much as I could while carrying my childhood on my back. We worked awfully hard on keeping the drugs out of his life. I was no angel. I had dabbled with marijuana and hash oil, but never really liked the lack of control so did not take up with it. I liked to have a drink once in awhile and I smoked cigarettes but only about 5 a day. Jay smoked over a pack a day. These vices stayed with us until after the kids were born. Jay quit first and I followed a little while later. We did not have liquor in our house unless we were going to have company. We did not allow drugs in our home nor smoking.

This was extremely hard on both of us as Jay's family thrived on all that. My family, not so much. We lived in St. Thomas until 1988. We moved to my parent's farm as my dad was having medical issues and my mom needed a hand. It was a great set up. We split the utilities and paid for our own groceries. My kids got to live with their grandparents as I had all my childhood. I pushed aside my memories there and jumped into helping my mom out. My dad was diagnosed in 1990 with three inoperable brain tumours. They gave him months to live. He had a shunt put in to divert the poisons from his head to his stomach cavity. From that surgery he contracted meningitis and was given a death sentence. Eight surgeries and seven had died. He remembered hearing a doctor say, 'this one isn't going to make it either'. He did and he lived until 1993. They said he would never walk again. He did with my mom, my sisters and I working daily with him. They said he would never drive again. He did, and within 3 months of surgery. I gave him my faith and allowed him to take my son, Josh with him down to the gas station. People asked me if that were safe, and I would tell them I had complete trust that my dad would protect my son.

I am so glad that I had forgiven my dad before he passed away. No, he died not knowing about the boarder. And after dad died, I decided I would never tell my mom. One day I may discuss this with my sister, Beth, but I do not think I will. Why bring up bad memories for her. If she ever wanted to, she would reach out to me. Besides the boarder, my sister and I were almost assaulted by her best friend's husband to be. He came to our farmhouse the night of his stag and they were getting married the next weekend. My parents never locked their door so in he came. I am sure my parents just figured it was one of the boys. He came upstairs and the first room he went into was my brother Roger's. We heard my brother yell 'Get out of my room you *asshole*!' He then came to our room. Once he entered, he came to my bedside. He was trying to climb into my bed and my sister told him to leave me alone. He then went to her bed and was trying to climb in hers. I heard her tell him to get out and go sleep it off on the couch downstairs. He did not get anywhere with my sister but chose to sit on the edge of her bed and masturbate. Gross. Once he was finished, he went downstairs. I cannot remember if he slept on the couch or left. Gladly I did not care. Again, my sister and I did not talk about it.

But it sure brought back memories for me. I was around thirteen when that happened. I started having nightmares again for awhile. I moved my bed around to try and send the nightmares somewhere else.

When my dad took ill, and we knew he was on borrowed time I had so much going through my head. I started writing again especially when I was sitting in the hospital on his many visits. I could feel his thoughts and I could hear others. I wrote for them and for my dad. I vividly remember one of his last visits, sitting on the floor at the windows beyond his bed and feeling someone with me. I wrote what I felt on a piece of paper in my purse as I had forgotten my notebook. It was surreal yet I was not thinking about what I was writing. Just let the words flow. I went home and when I pulled out the paper and read what I had written it was like the first time I had seen this one.

I LOVE YOU DAD – GOODBYE

Have I told you lately, how much you mean to me?
And that you've taught me to be the best that I can be!

I still can remember from when I was very young
To always carry on until the day was done.

You said to always smile at everyone you meet
To always stay happy even though it's a hard feat.

I've always tried hard to do what you wanted me to
Even though it doesn't look it, it's the best that I can do.

I'll always love you dearly, not just because you are my DAD
But because you've loved me even when you were tired and sad.

It really is hard for me to let go of you now.
But it was you who taught me, so I do know how.

I promise to try hard, so of me you'll be proud
And I'll live life as you taught me for as long as I'm allowed

As I kiss you goodbye, even though it makes me sad
I'll always remember you were the best DAD for me to have.

I LOVE YOU DAD

TOBY
KAL 17/05/22

I wrote many little poems while sitting at my Dad's bedside. They just poured out and some were happy, but most were on the sad side.

GOD WAITS FOR ME

The road might be long – he waits for me.
It's always weary – but, God is there for me.
Troubles are always there – and he believes in me.
My eyes might be teary – yet, God waits for me.

And when I pray – God listens to me.
I may not hear him answer – but, he's there for me.
When life seems too much – he's still there for me.
I offer him a prayer – and God listens to me.

Thru all of my life – he waits for me.
Even when I don't believe – yet, God is there for me.
In health and in sickness – and he is there for me.
He knows and tries to relieve – he still waits for me.

And at the end of the line – God waits for me.
I can see a bend in the road – and he's there for me.
I know all is well – because God's here for me.
He takes from me my load – God believed in me.

TOBY

So, I made sure from then I always carried my notebook and would write what I felt. Sometimes there was nothing and sometimes it flowed. A couple of days before dad passed sitting in his room again by myself, I felt his pain again. I held his hand, and he squeezed my hand although he was not awake. Here was my daddy. I was his princess as a young child and would sit on his lap to eat supper. I sang with my dad quite often as he was always singing in the car, on the tractor, in the barn. Anywhere he went he had a joke, and he had a song. He was talented but never had anyone tell him to run with it.

My dad had a photographic memory as well as my brother Phyllip. I was missing my dad already.

So, I sat and just listened to the sound of the hospital with my eyes closed. I heard muffled talking. I felt sad. My heart hurt and my fingers reached for my notebook. This was eerie and I did not feel afraid.

After I was done writing I read over what I had in front of me. It resounded within my soul, and I honestly felt it was dad telling me everything would be fine. What a wonderful thought to have. What a gift he gave me. I do not know if he could read my thoughts all jumbled within my own head, but I didn't feel sad.

A few days later, Dad passed away, but he hung on as long as he could. Dad was surrounded by most of us kids and grandkids. We sat around telling jokes and reminiscing. My mom told my dad she was leaving to go to a friend's anniversary party, and he had her permission to go. She kissed him and left. He waited for her to return and shortly after took his final breath. We hugged each other and sat quietly mourning his passing, but knowing he was out of pain and that made us feel better. So, I gave this poem to our minister to use at dad's funeral. He used parts of it and that made me know dad heard it.

I have to say my dad was late for everything. And the family used to laugh and say he is going to be late for his own funeral. My dad was buried on April fools' day. That was so befitting of my dad. He was a Joker he could recite jokes at the drop of a hat and his repertoire was immense when it came to jokes. The funeral director at about 40 minutes after the funeral was supposed to be finally said we must get going on this and there were still lineups of people that had not been able to get inside the building. The Chapel was full all three or four viewing areas were full the downstairs was full out the door and around the side of the building into the parking lot was full. It was a wonderful thing to say the least. The honor these people did to my dad was heart warming. Since it was a cold blustery day, our family asked that people just go back to our church not come to the grave site. But there we were heading out to the grave site with a line of cars miles long. We stood around where dad was being buried and the minister did his service there. He asked if anyone had anything else to say. A few people spoke up to honor dad. And then we stood there in silence and out from behind the headstone which everybody was around came a cat no one had seen before now. And it took off through the crowd and into a field. My mom said, 'well that's fitting he's going fishing, I guess'. And then the minister asked anymore thoughts. My youngest son, Josh, shook his head and mustered up saying bbbbrrrrr and we all went to our vehicles and headed back to the church. It was nice to hear all the stories from the old folks about my dad when he was younger. When he played checkers and he umpired, and he did all that and everybody gave their wishes. The next couple of days reading all the sympathy cards was touching. My dad was a well-known well-liked man, and I was fortunate to call him dad.

They say I died last night; you know.
> I don't believe them, but they say it's so.
If I died, I would have felt something,
> Even a little pain, but I felt nothing.

How can they tell if I'm really gone?
> Did they run all the tests? They could be wrong.
Look at me! If I'm dead, why do I feel so awake?
> Tell them for me – I'm alive, for goodness' sake.

Why do you stand there, not making a sound?
> Do you even realize I'm around?
I guess I didn't ask what was your name?
> Did they say you were dead too? Is it a game?

Gee, I wish I knew where I am now?
> Do you know? Can you tell me? Are you allowed?
I can't stand this; I've got to get away.
> I've got things to do, I'll come back another day.

When I come back, who should I ask for?
> Pardon me? Excuse me? Could you tell me once more?
You mean I'm really gone; I can't go home?
> I have to, please, I feel so all alone.

Well, I guess I was wrong, and they were right!
> I really did die late last night.
And all along you've been right by my side.
> You came yourself to be my guide.

I feel so light, as light as can be.
> As if, for once, my soul has been set free.
So, I'll go with you, and I'll argue no more.
> I really don't know what I was worried for.

Onward we go to peace everlasting.
> There's no turning back, no need for grieving.
Thank you, God, for seeing me through
> I'm ready to start life anew.

TOBY
(I love you Dad)

I have always wanted to explore who I really was. I know I tucked me away to be safe as a child and the person I am today is the protector. I hear her voice at odd times. She yells out sometimes or makes presence known in a more subtle way. She may linger for a while, or she may attach herself to me until I recognize she is there.

I am an enabler; I am a soft touch. I have too big a heart. I have so much difficulty saying no to a sob story. I fought hard to be a strong, mindful woman. I wanted others to see a stoic, smart person when they looked at me. The problem was I was not strong. Inside I was frightened that someone might see the insecure child I kept away, find out her story and judge me as bad. I honestly believed I had taken care of being afraid when I was ten, but slowly I realized she was still there. This makes sense more to me now. Every sob story I heard would bring a little of her out. She could not control what happened to her, but she broke me inside and I tried so hard to help others that needed to be heard or helped.

Now in retrospect I know if I had had an outlet to release all the pent-up trauma, I might have been a different person. I had dreams I never followed through on. I was not strong. The shadow on the wall controls my strength.

As I walk this earth I can plainly see
Many people are looking back at me
    I've tried to see within their smiles
    But to me some look like deep, dark souls

There are a few that when I meet
I can see what it is that they do seek
    Others I can feel all their pain
    And yet I can't help keep away tears of rain

It pains my heart when I seem to fail
To lessen their load and let ships sail
    Yet I continue on smiling throughout
    At some point I will see what they are about

I pray to God to guide me on my way
And help me to be there all through their days
    Those who I only see their backs staring back at me
    I will ask God to help them and open their eyes to see

KAL 17/05/07

LET'S TALK 4-H

In 4H we usually had a floating secretary, and I was fascinated with seeing different girls take notes and add their own flair to our minutes. I found a happy place just reading how different each girl was. I was always asked to write up a 'Me' page as I had the best descriptions to put into the reader's mind who we all were. And I loved writing and composing. There lies my passion. Writing. Composing. Creating. I can lose myself within poetry and words. Glimpses of 'all of me' comes out there. Glimpses of others also.

"ME" PAGE

What do you get when you take members and have them all take turns writing up a meeting? You get "ME" – a floating secretary!

There are so many qualities and personalities that I consist of, I really don't know where to begin:

I laugh and I cry.
I can be sneaky or shy.
I'm usually polite.
Unless it's the wrong night.
I'm married; I'm single.
I like to mingle.
I'm earnest and/or efficient.
Then again, I can be different.
That's my one side, now the other.
For one thing I'm sure – I do have a mother.
Brown, blue, grey or green.
I've got the prettiest eyes you've ever seen.
Brown, black, blonde or red.
Take your pick for upon my head.
Short, tall, medium or small
That's complete and describes my all.

As you can see, I am a well-rounded person. And now the big question – Would you like to meet me??!?

TOBY

Also, in 4H, we had to introduce ourselves and I hated the standard form with your information such as name, address, telephone, how many clubs you have taken, why you took this one, etc. So, I tried a few different methods over the years, and these tell a little story rather than bore you to tears. I know my Home Economist always looked forward to my club book. She said it was refreshing to read more into a member. I recall once telling her that she would be shocked if I let loose. We laughed; I walked away thinking 'if she only knew!'.......

ME2

You want my outlook on myself, euh? Everyone knows it is a difficult subject. Sure, you can give your name, address, and personal interest. But how can one truthfully write about oneself.

I always go with the adage: "Seeing is believing." Unless it's magic or television, that is. It's hard in another way. You think you know who, what, where and why you are, then, all of a sudden you don't.

Sure, I know my name and that I'm a married woman (even though I still feel like a child in some matters), with four beautiful (but somewhat mischievous) children and a loving husband. I have a great family (I mean my parents mostly). They are always there when I need them.

It's true, though, that's not me. I mean it is me, but then again it isn't. I'm a whole different person each day. Sure, my looks change gradually, it's what I feel inside that's changing all the time. I love, yet I can hate (such a cruel word); I laugh, yet I can cry. I give, though, I will take (sometimes I just can't take anything). I'm such a complex person as is everyone. No one is just simply a person. They are always changing.

So, I'm going to keep my eyes and ears open. I don't want to miss a thing. Oh, oh – I'm changing again........................!

TOBY

ME

You say you want to know about me –
　　Well, there isn't much to say.
But I love to talk about me.
　　Doesn't everyone feel that way?

I have many different qualities.
　　I can be moody, calm or shy.
I can be stable on the outside
　　But my feelings I might hide.

Four beautiful children have I
    A husband whom I love very much.
A family who are very caring.
    I couldn't be happier with a life as such.

I don't care if we haven't a lot of money
    Because it could never buy
Someone calling you Mommy or Honey
    Or hugging you when you cry.

I think I can say I like myself
    Because self-esteem means a lot.
It's hard to talk about myself
    But I gave it my best shot.

TOBY

I think I can remember the pledge still:

I pledge:

My head to clearer thinking,
My heart to greater loyalty
My hands to larger service
My heart to better living
For my club, my community and my country.

Some clubs added and my world at the end. In my time at 4-H we
stopped at country.
Achievement Day

Good evening, Miss Wilson, fellow 4-Hers and guests

It's the night of Achievement Day and in our prepared skit
All Corinth members have gathered to portray our charm and wit
We have a few traditional breads from around the world for you
So, sit back, relax, and listen there's nothing for you to do.
First Kim Pressey from Mexico bears Zuni Cornbread for all to eat
Wouldn't you just love to taste it, myself, I cannot wait.
Now here's Carrie Godby from France with French Bread as you can
see.

So temptingly delicious and she bakes so well, mais qui?
Lenora Pressey came over from Germany with Pretzels freshly baked.
But be careful when making this recipe for everyone's goodness' sake.
Next there's Angela Smith from England, Wholegrain English
Muffins came with her. So easy to make and nutritious for you, you'll
serve them for breakfast for sure. Karyn Pressey came from Ireland
bringing her famous Irish Freckle Bread. Delicious, nutritious, and
economical too, serve this to our guests and they'll be well fed. These
are our Traditional Breads from around the world, there's only one
more thing we wish to say.

So, from me, Kim Kitchenham and all the rest, "Merry Christmas to
all and have a nice day!"

TOBY 1979

I really enjoyed writing during this time. It was a great way to release my inner thoughts a little. It was also a great time to be near my Mom. She really knew so much about almost everything.

I spent a lot of time in my formative years isolating from people as much as possible. One reason was how I felt about myself. Another reason was how I felt when I was around others. I tied in with their feelings.

Honestly, I remember when I was around sixteen my brother had a party. There Jeff was, a friend of his that I had went out with a couple times (well hooked up with if we are truthful). He came in and everywhere I went in the house, there he was. After an hour or so he came over and asked if I wanted to take a run into town in his Camaro. I remember laughing and saying, 'maybe later.' So as soon as he was looking away, I ducked out the back door through a bunch of guys smoking weed, out the door into our garage and snuck out a side door no one really knew about. I slipped behind the house and hid behind a snowbank beside a tool shed. There I was feeling smart and satisfied that I gave Jeff the slip. I looked around the corner and Jeff was standing in the light of the open garage door looking around, so I ducked back behind the shed and kept completely silent. I did not move an inch when I heard a noise behind me and there, smiling was Jeff. I made an excuse that I was taking a pee and a break from all the noise. He grabbed my hand and away we went to his car. As we were pulling out, I saw my parents returning home with a concerned look on their face. They had no idea there was a party planned at our house. I am sure the kids cleared out quick after that. My gramps, though, made sure my dad knew he was okay with the party. And a bunch of my brother's friends hung around and were still there when I got back home. But I just knew he would find me…. he always did. I knew when he was at a party or hotel before I could see him. I just felt his presence. I never loved Jeff, but he was okay. I think he could feel me too. In another lifetime we were together or at least family.

EACH OTHER'S ARMS

Here this night, I sit thinking,
About the times we had been together
In each other's arms.
There were some good and some bad times,
But we'll remember them all.

The first time I was with you
We were not alone.
Surrounded by friends, all in all.
The swim refreshed us,
the drink together us brought.
But the night found us
In each other's arms.
You didn't demand and I didn't ask.
We just knew what was right and wrong.

The months went by before we met again.
But you were different and I the same
You demanded and I didn't ask.
We still found solace
In each other's arms.

More months passed, a new year was here
Before we met again under new stars.
The dance was lovely, the drive beautiful
Again, we were
In each other's arms.
Me telling you my problems
You solving.
Oh, how you gave me reassurance.

There were many times after that,
We were alone.
Loving each other,
In each other's arms.
But though you have moved
Far from here,
I'll never forget being
In each other's arms.

TOBY

Jeff was one of the guys in my life as he just always showed up when I was not feeling great about myself. Yes, he was just a quick and noncommittal lay, what would be considered friends with benefits now. The last time we got together I told him I was in love with someone, but it was only a one-way avenue. He listened, he held me, he did not even try to go any further. He took me home and told me he really hoped whoever this jerk was would realize the catch he could have. I think I heard something along that line a couple times from guys I considered friends. I did not realize until later that he might have loved me, and I walked away from his car that night. Funny at that point in my life who I was in love with was one of his best friends. And I would have gone to the end of the earth if he would just noticed me as a love interest. That is a story for later.

I do know he was always showing up in my life and we had a weird connection. So long ago, yet fresh in one's mind. I pray Jeff has had a great life. He moved to Alberta shortly after our last meeting.

SMILE WITHOUT A SOUND

How did you notice me through all the crowd?
I wasn't making a sound cause the music was loud.

You approached me with a smile.
I wonder if you know what I thought all the while?

Unbearable thoughts kept going through my mind.
If you walked away that would suit me fine.

And when the music began to slow down,
You asked me to dance I didn't make a sound.

And when you turned to find someone new,
I knew that we both had taken our proper cue.
Goodbye love and see you around,
When I see you again I'll just smile without a sound.

TOBY

I had a fast and furious teenage life. I went from 'church camp' Kim to 'Little Deano' to who knows what anymore. I know I wanted to feel loved, and I wanted to find love. I wished for each guy I went out with to be the last. Well, there were a couple that I knew were not going to be the last, but only a couple. When I met my first husband it was a whirlwind. I know my parents were sure it was just a phase. Even my minister, in front of him, told me it would not work with my background and his lack of background. But I loved him. He got me. We fit together. I had just reunited with my high school sweetheart, Steve, for about the 12th time. I was never sure he was committed to just me. I had been dating a guy, Romi, who I saw about 4 times a year. So, Jay was a little bit of fresh air. Or maybe the bad boy, although I am sure he was just lost.

Jay was the first person I talked about some of my past. We discussed everything. How many people we had dated? Dark secrets, which included my dark shadow in my life. How I blamed my own dad for not protecting me. He knew how many guys I thought was the one. Jay knew the names of the ones that captured my heart even more. I knew the names of the girls that hurt him over the years. I knew he had no schooling to speak of. He told me how he carved a girl's initials into his arm and almost bled to death. His family were nothing like mine. They had a bad history in St. Thomas from mostly his generation. His gramma was a matriarch and when she passed so did the integrity of the family. His brother, Steve was one of the purse snatchers from the 70's along with one of the fire chief's son, Larry.

How could we make it? I was determined to make it work and we could have if I did not tangle with the shadow so much and lose my way a bit. I wish he had stood up and been determined to make it work but that was not his forte. But if we had worked it all out, I never would have met my second husband, John. I would not have exposed myself to the world and start to try and heal. So many what ifs in our lives. So many roads that could have been taken.
There were a couple times before Jay, and I wed 7 months after we met that I called it off. Even a couple of weeks before we wed. But we clung to each other in a way that gave us meaning. As each of our four children were born, I thought we had made it and would be okay. That changed and I can imagine it was when my dad was diagnosed with inoperable brain tumors. Cancer, the 'C' word. My little happy corner was being upheaved from the core. I had always thought I might tell my parents one day when we were all old and

grey and laugh about the shadow on the wall. I know I had promised myself I would never ever tell my parents but as I aged, I thought they had a right to know why I was such a difficult teenager. I put them through hell.

Well Cancer took that option away. I would no way tell them when my dad was sick. And after my dad lost his fight with Cancer, I told myself I would never tell my mother as she had already been through so much. Do not get me wrong, my mom was a tough old bird with a stamina and heart of pure strength. But why bring up any bad this late in the game.

Why exactly…. well for me I need to release the fear, the hate, the shame, the rage. And more than anything else I need to forgive. Not for him, but for me. Ignite Your Heart has taught me that. I knew I needed to, but I still have some residual darkness hanging in my heart and that shadow creeps in occasionally.

What am I doing here?
Have I figured that out yet?
What can I do while I'm here?
Has it all been laid and set?
    If I worry about this all the time
    Will I remember who I am?
    If I think about what I've missed
    Will I just cry here where I stand?
I'm hurting deep inside my soul
Can I handle all this pain?
I look around and feel so alone
Could this alone drive me insane?
    Time isn't going fast enough
    Why is that I need to know?
    I slowly lose a part of myself
    Will I know which way to go?
Why am I crying by myself
While my tears fall to the ground?
When will I be able to just go home
And feel again me – safe and sound?

KAL 17/04/23

There were many times as a child and teenager I would find myself feeling blue, a bit sorry for myself and write down why I did not deserve to live. I would walk to the woods at the end of our property. I was unafraid of any wild animals. I could not have cared less if there was a child abductor lurking about the dark underbrush. I might crawl up in the old chicken barn on the old straw and talk to no one about why I was so unhappy. I would ask God why I had been born. I would demand answers to why no one cared about me. I might shake my fist at the world and swear a blue streak into the void of the barn. I wandered our property a lot. I envisioned what my family would be like if I had never been born. I would question if I really existed or was I in someone else's nightmare. I could even think I was adopted and passed off as family. Many times, I searched photos and never, ever were their photos of my mom pregnant before I had been born. Was I born? Did I exist?

I was so mad at the world, at God, at life, at death! I wanted death, but not to myself, to my life. I wanted to have a chance to start over and be better. To make my family proud. I wanted to be that friend everyone loved to see. Even as a child I felt different. I heard my older family members talking about who would be stuck with me. I knew I did not have any close friends. I had friends at school. I had friends at church. I had friends of the family. But I did not have that friend you just knew you would have forever, and I was no one's forever friend either.

If I had never been would life be the same
If I had never been would anyone be the better
If I had never been would they be any different
If I had never been would they care about each other?

If I had been born a moment in time later
Would I be me or would I be someone I know
If I had been born on a different day or year
Would I be someone I'd want to know?

If I could change how my life has gone so far
Would it have made any different to them?
If I could have loved someone else
Would they all stand there to condemn?

If I could, would I then be me or not
If I would, then could I stand up and try
If I did and they didn't, would it make sense
If I could live, would I or would I just die?

KAL 2015/06/02

We lived in the country, and you did not go to friend's house to sleep
over. You did not have the chance to play together everyday. At
school you played with kids but knew you would be going home, and
they would go to theirs. I remember going with my mom to
her childhood friend's house who had kids my age. I really liked her
two oldest daughters and thought here were childhood friends. We
went a few times. They moved and we still visited a few more
times then they moved, and my mom was sad because no one knew
they had moved and no one knew where. Years later my mom told
me that her friend's husband was violent and that is why no one knew
where. He abused her and he was starting to hurt the girls. She had
taken her three daughters and fled. Apparently, he had shown up late
one night at our farmhouse demanding to know if my mom knew
where she had gone. My dad set him straight and showed him the
door. Told him to get sober and find a life. I think about them and
think my parents always knew where they were and did not let anyone
know where to protect them. Possibly my parents were the ones to
convince her to get away.

I tried to be friends with the kids I went to school and
church with, but it got hard as I liked kids that did not go to church
with us, and they did not want to be close friends with them
so always made it a dilemma for me. If I played with the other kids,
they would be standoffish with me and if I spent time together with
my church friends the other kids would alienate me for a while.
I could not understand why people could not all get along. I quite
often ended up hanging with the guys, usually the older guys. They
were easier to understand. And in public school you were safe it was
not about sex, but sports. Also, guys are easier to talk to. None of
that schoolgirl *crap* that happens. You know – I like you, no I do not,
did you hear about Susie…...? I heard Marjorie did this…. If you
don't play the game, I want to I won't be your friend anymore. If you
talk to her do not talk to me. I will tell everyone you eat your boogers

if you don't play with only me. Yes, it gets that serious and yet ridiculous.

But that gets away from how I felt when I was by myself out in the field, or in the woods or in the hay mow. I remember wandering the property a lot. I now wonder if anyone ever wondered where I was when I was wandering. I have always liked being away from other humans and only surrounded by God's earth and cows and dogs. I loved talking with our cows and our dogs. They listened and never once interrupted.

When I was curiously letting go with abandonment of life itself within the woods, I was safe in my thoughts. I was not the victim. I could not care less if there was any danger around me. I saw myself as in control of the day. I felt that nature could watch over me. I was in tune with it. Some may find it strange, but I could feel how the woods felt. The trees, the moss, the trilliums, the skunk cabbage, everything. I could sit quietly with my eyes closed and know when a butterfly would fly around me. My safe place and I could not go there a lot, but I did go as much as I could. If I could not go there, I could be found up in the old hay loft. There was a wonderful place for me.

Up in the hay loft, sitting or laying on the hay. I could stare out at the fields where the cows would graze. There were birds, bees, butterflies flying in and out of the open side. Sometimes the family dog would climb up and sit with me. That was comforting. It was there I would plan my life out. Back then I would have a short life. I imagined I would not live past sixteen. I would see how I would end up and see how others would act. I even thought up ways I could commit suicide and not make it hard on my parents. It was in the hayloft that I started writing poetry and songs. That saved me from conducting any plans of death. Well, that and the dog. If that dog could talk, I would have been committed, I am sure.

SPINNING LIKE A TOP

Spinning like a top, my life continues on.
I'm up, I'm down. I hear an endless sound.

Finding it so hard to balance myself today.
Yesterday was better; tomorrow come what may.

Spinning like a top, my life continues on.
I'm up, I'm down. I hear an endless sound.

Wanting to do more with my time at hand
Searching around me, where will I land?

Spinning like a top, my life continues on.
I'm up, I'm down. I hear an endless sound.

Seeing it all through, up to the very end.
Believing I'm okay until the angels are sent.

Spinning like a top, my life continues on.
I'm up, I'm down. I hear an endless sound.

KAL 17/09/23

I wondered why I felt alone even though there was never a person in our home. It was the hub of community activity. My parents were well loved by all. They sacrificed so much to take care of us children and grandparents. I wish I knew more of how they felt at the same time. I always wondered if they thought they had not been there for me. I know they did not know what had happened to me, but I always envisioned they did but did not want to upset me in case I may have forgotten about it all.

Our family, including the many that came to our house, was busy. I hid secrets of others that I knew on the farm. I saw a lot, although I stopped talking about it when it happened to me too. I knew the haymow was a busy, sexual place. Cousins, friends, and such spent a lot of time in there. It was child exploration mostly, but we still learnt a lot from each other. When summer was in full swing, there was the local swimming holes. Irrigation ponds on farms but loved by everyone in the community. Bathing suits were not required. I was safe as my older cousins protected me from the advances of younger boys. My brothers even would make me go in the water then take off my suit and throw it on the bank. No boys were allowed to get close to me while naked. When we were done swimming one of my brothers would grab my suit and throw it to me. Try as I may to get close to certain guys, my brothers or cousins would not let any of them close.

I was okay with this. There were times I wished my brothers would just worry about themselves and a few of the friends were kind of cute. Now and then I could swim into the reeds and steal a quick kiss from one of them. I was infatuated with a couple and a few times I would go and meet them at the pond at night. Sexual exploration was fun. I am not upset that I experimented with these boys. It taught me a lot and helped take away my fears of sex with guys. The shadow diminished each time. I was not ashamed of learning more about sex and love this way. It helped me know the difference between the two. Although I may have thought I loved a couple of them, I knew it was just sex. Funny that the only guy that used protection was the one guy I would have loved to have spent my life with. And I guess lucky I was not a young single mother as there were quite a few experimentations in sex.

I've opened my eyes to everything
    And still, I cannot quite see.
Where it is I've just come from
    Or where is home for me?

Did you know you were my lifeline?
    Did you know you've seen me thru?
I didn't realize all of this
    Until I thought of losing you.

Maybe now it's time for me to say
    It's my turn to now help you.
Is it any wonder we seemed confused
    When we don't know exactly what to do?

Pain has caused grief to you and I
    Yet we struggle on and seem to be
Getting thru it all together
    Maybe your home is here with me?

I'll close my eyes to everything
    And just see if I can really see
Where it is I'm now heading for
    Are you my love, my home for me?

KAL 03/21/96

But as much as I tried to banish the shadow to oblivion by being a free spirit, it would rear its ugly head. It did not help when he would show up with his family at the farmhouse. I made every excuse to get out of being home when they were there. And I would look for anything and anyone to get out of the house. Good thing there was always something to do in our area. So many hotels within a fifteen-minute drive and many single males looking for someone to talk (and more) too. Having many different friends always gave me somewhere to be also. Thank God I had friends that were older and could go out all the time. I know that I was running away from confrontation. And I was substituting different guys yearning for someone to just love me for me. I still do not know exactly who I am. So many questions still inside of me and here I am in the twilight of my life. Back to 1970's…. The seventies were much better than the sixties for free love. We did not do all the drugs that the sixty's did but could match up with someone and go on our way. There was only one regret in all my teenage life and that was hooking up with a hockey friend of my brother's and getting crabs, yes crabs, from him. I told my mom it had to be from the toilets at the ball diamond, but I knew where I got them as I had not been with anyone for over a month and bang, there were little *buggers*. I picked off about twelve of them before I yelled for my mom. She did not believe me until I showed her the Kleenex with them squirming around. We had lice medicine and I did my first shave and went back to baby fresh bottom. Gone in 30 seconds. Yeah. I kept myself bald for a few months. First and last time.

I did hook up with another of my brother's friends shortly after and he was overly excited that I shaved myself. Was a great night parking down a dirt road, windows down so we could hear the crickets until the mosquitos found our asses…. that was not great. But again, this was a guy I really liked for a long time as he played baseball with my brother for years and I was so excited when he asked me to go for a late-night drive after spending the evening laying on my bed trying to entice me to go. I played hard to get for a little bit. Man was he a cutie. He is still cute but that was a lifetime ago and he never asked me out once he got what he wanted. Why were guys like that?

It isn't normal to think like this
But it's been so long since our last kiss
I try not to give into all those thoughts
Then doubts arise inside of me a lot

Crazy ideas start to form in my head
Should I believe that our love is dead?
It starts to eat away at my trust
Soon all that will be left is dry dust

Days are hard but the nights eat at me
Dreams become nightmares that I see
I want to turn off all that is inside
Pull up my blanket and away to hide

So far away and all by myself
I take out my heart and put it on a shelf
It hurts too much to think anymore
My heart is gone, and my head is sore

It isn't normal for me here any more
All windows are shut and also the door
No freedom or love is within my grasp
I'm giving up; and love fades too fast

KAL 17/06/02

I had so many doubts about who I was. I had no confidence really. I hated how I looked. I did not believe in myself. I will be honest if some guy had pulled up in front of our house and promised the moon if I left with him right then, I would have grabbed my toothbrush and jumped in. That was my self worth at that time of my life. It never really got much better through life, but I did start to know how to make others believe I was confident. I would mask myself all day long, come home, go to bed, and toss and turn because I hated having to wear a mask.

You know all my life everyone treated me like a child. I was married and in labour and my sister and sister-in-law stood at the door looking in after making a bet that I would yell and cry while delivering my first child. I knew they were waiting there. Waiting for me to lose it. Waiting to say I could not manage being an adult and having a baby. So, I bit my tongue and not once did I yell out or swear or anything. Not that I did not want to, but I was not going to give anyone more fuel to the child fire.

I am the youngest and I got away with a lot of stuff because I was an excellent crier. Well, they taught me to. They encouraged me to cry otherwise why did they constantly prod me to cry. Bull frog, Pete, stick your bottom lip out just a little bit more if you are going to pout. Stop crying just because you are wrapped up in blankets and we will not let you out. (I was suffocating) I always wondered if they were not pushing me to see if I would disappear. How can one become an adult when everyone treats you like you are a child? At family get togethers my ideas were never good enough to follow. I would sit in the background most of my life. I even was just a backup harmonizer for my sister. I had a lot of songs inside of me and I could sing, except when I was around family. I never pushed to have anyone hear my songs. Well, my Mom heard them, and I did let my sister hear some, but as I'd play one for her, she'd be busy doing stuff around her house and I honestly don't think she listened to what she heard. Okay pity party is over at my house. I have played the violin enough and no one complained, nor did they join.

I want to be the funny one. I want others to hear me when I speak. I want to bring smiles to everyone I meet. I want to love me. I do not know how to do that, I fear. I want to learn how to love me. I do not feel I am able to get over that hump. I want to allow myself to learn to love me. I think I am strong enough to examine myself and see why I don't love myself. I know the mistakes I have made in my life.

FAMILY

When you think it's impossible
    to go back home again.
Think again. Be brave.
    Go back on the track you've lain.
People who care and love you
    don't care if the road was wrong.
Care again. Be brave.
    They've loved you all along.

    Family should be your closest friends.
    Family should love you until the end.
    Family is important, they're always there.
    Family stand behind you when life isn't fair.

When you've tried all you can
    and there isn't anything left to do,
Try again, Be brave.
    They'll open arms of love for you
Friends and family don't turn their backs
    to the people they really love.
Turn around again. Be brave.
    God watches you from above.

    Family should be your closest friends.
    Family should love you until the end.
    Family is important, they're always there.
    Family stand behind you when life isn't fair.

TOBY 07/22/95

I have asked God and myself to forgive me. I just do not know if I can forgive myself totally. I know I need to allow others to forgive me. I know I have forgiven so many people in my life, but I still have the shadow lurking even though I have tried to forgive him. I have a lot of "I's" in this paragraph. So, let us try this…. I forgive you for taking my innocence. I forgive you for making me doubt myself for the rest of my life. I forgive you for taking away the feeling of trusting people. I forgive you for stealing the safety of my bed, my bedroom, my house. I forgive you for the feeling that my parents let me down. Will he ever hear this from me or read this? I doubt it but I've given this to the universe, and I do hope I can get the fog out of my head that had plagued me for so many years. God, I hope I can start healing at least a little part of me now.

Here I am a child at heart
Pretending to be grown up and, oh so smart.
When all the time I want to be
Young and happy and, ah yes, carefree.

People expect me to do my best
To keep on smiling, though, is the hardest.
You can only do so much you know.
And then before you're done it's time to go.

When I was a child, it wasn't so difficult.
But now I'm older – I'm always at fault.
I'm expected to be patient and content
To be mature – but I just can't.

Is it possible to be a youthful adult?
Can you be mature with a childish jolt?
Will others respect your humorous self?
Or shall I just keep my thoughts to myself?

I've decided that it is best to be me
And everyone will have to accept that, you see.
I enjoy the simple things that make me smile
I'll be happy with a flair of my own style.

KAL 04/20/13

My ever-recurring dream of running hard at public school and I jump and fly into the air and as long as I keep running, I stay up above everyone. I have that one so many times. Sometimes I fly down and swoop over kids that would ridicule me. Sometimes I just keep flying higher and higher and soon everyone is just a pinpoint below me. Tiny little ants milling about. There are a few where I suddenly fall and just before I hit the earth, I awaken and am safe in my bed. I have tried to figure out what each means and why I have them sporadically. I try to think what my life is at when I do and what this dream may to reflecting upon. Have not figured it out yet but I do dream in colour. And I have many repetitive dreams. Maybe on another platform of earth I am this other person? Or it is alerting me to something about to happen? I will figure it all out someday.

I dreamt I was soaring high above the clouds
And I flew as high as my breath would allow
    As I looked down to earth I couldn't clearly see
    Anyone or anything that meant something to me
I was upset with this, but I kept soaring on
Hoping that I would understand as I flew along
    My dream suddenly changed, and I was looking at home
    Everything was changed too and inside no one I've known
I turned around and looked and then I did see
People I knew and loved were just staring through me
    I tried to talk to each as they walked right by
    No one answered my voice, I couldn't think why
So, I flew again into the sky and tried to find me
But alas, I am now gone this is what is to be
    I dreamt I was standing by our dear Lord up above
    He told me I was home, and I would always be loved.

KAL 17/05/12

Many times, in life I have asked God what is happening to me. I do have faith that there is a God. And I know someday I will meet up with those who have left me already. God has been a rock for me. I have held many prayers up to Him. And I have confided already for any wrongs I have done and any insecurities I have.

I feel the pain, it brings on the burn
I sit and wonder when is it my turn?
I trust in You to guide me today.
I know it'll be fine, and I will go Your way.

No matter how hard it has been I go on
No sorrow, no shame as I sing Your song.
I have come this far; I won't turn around.
I will continue thru if I am allowed

The pain swells up, the tears fall down
The body shakes so, and there's no one around.
My mind is all Yours, I will stay the stead.
I won't turn back now regardless of what's said.

KAL 02/10/15

Life plays cruel tricks on us and no matter what you do, you fall into a crevice and spend years crawling out. Do not ever get me wrong, I loved my family, and I could never imagine having any other children then the ones I have. I am proud of the adults they have become (mostly, but they are still learning about life – we all are). I was in love with my first husband, and I am deeply in love with my husband now. He just makes sense to me. We make sense. We make each other laugh and we make each other shake our heads. I would never want to be with anyone else but him. John is a wonderful, warm, loving, smart man. He is just a man, but he is my heart.

You gave me back my life
When you asked me to be your wife
You make each day brighter
And make my load lighter.
Loving you is so very easy
And you set my heart free

    Stay with me baby
    Never leave me alone
    Hold me tight baby
    You are the best I've known.

You gave me your loving heart
And we promised to never part
You make me smile every day
When you just look my way.
Caring for you is so very right
When you hold me every night.

    Stay with me baby
    Never leave me alone
    Hold me tight baby
    You are the best I've known.

KAL 04/08/13

As life jumps around so does what affects a person each day. A trigger. It may be a sound or a smell or déjà vu. Whatever it is I have masked my emotions when something does that. I tell jokes or just sit quietly and smile. I find talking to someone hard to do, by that I mean talking to a professional. It is easier to just have a conversation with someone and listen to what is going on in their own life. Many times, I can agree with their feelings as they are the same as mine. I try to help people feel more comfortable in theirs.

I smile as I have aged when someone cannot believe that a person can go through pain, grief, turmoil, trauma, exploitation, hatred, narcissistic horror, so much and still stand in front of another and find love. This only means, that a person has the ability to still have a morsel of trust. And those that cannot get past all that are still struggling with the depth of the trauma. They have not been given the coping tools yet. Years ago, you buried it and struggled on praying and hoping life is better than what you experienced. Now there are so many agencies and professionals that are trained to help. I smile because I survived a small trauma and I made it through life. I helped many on my path because I love to listen to others. When I listen, I grow. When I see, I mend. There are so many people in our world that have had a much harder life and their pain is so much more than I could even imagine.

When I cry, I cry because I know they are out there. I know they may have a support system that they have pushed away, or they have no one. There are not enough tears to shed for those without support. If you are reading this and have any turmoil you have covered up because you were afraid to say anything, please reach out and talk to someone. Ask for help. Find out to whom to talk. Never think you are not worth it. You are and you need to release the pain and heartache. If you are living with someone who is hurting you emotionally, physically, or sexually, get out. Talk to your doctor, to a therapist, to a friend, to a neighbour, to a family member, to a minister. There are ways to safely leave. You matter. You are loved. You can love yourself also. That is perfectly all right.

I need to hear your voice
I need to see your smile
If only it was my choice
I'd cross over many miles

You are always on my mind
You are always on my thoughts
If you could cross the line
You'd see the love I've sought

We are joined within our hearts
We are one through all the years
If we hurt because we're apart
We'd know there's nothing to fear

Our love will stand the sands of time
Our love is strong and is true
If our love holds a tight line
Our love will get us through.

KAL 17/05/06

I have always been afraid to try and relay my feelings to others. I am okay to talk to anyone, but I sugar coat myself. I tell them what I think they want to hear. I agree with them and do not very often give my point of view. If I have said something and they come back to argue, I will back down. When I leave that person, I am so frustrated with myself. I ask myself over and over why don't you trust your knowledge over that person's point of view? I berate myself so much. I pray to God to help me do better. Help me feel the confidence to state what I feel aloud. I sit and wonder why I do not feel smart enough, cool enough, wise enough, stable enough…just enough. Those are the days I just feel exhausted and want to shrivel into a ball and disappear. I am comfortable if today was my last day. I welcome going home to Heaven and reuniting with my cherished loved ones that have gone before me.

I feel the pain, it brings on the burn
I sit and wonder when is it my turn?
I trust in You to guide me today.
I know it'll be fine, and I will go Your way.

No matter how hard it has been I go on
No sorrow, no shame as I sing Your song.
I have come this far; I won't turn around.
I will continue thru if I am allowed

The pain swells up, the tears fall down
The body shakes so, and there's no one around.
My mind is all yours, I will stay the stead.
I won't turn back now regardless of what's said.

KAL 02/10/15

But if I live another day, week, month, year I am okay with that. I want to be here to help my grandchildren through all their trials and tribulations. I want to be a safe spot for them. I love them to pieces, and I hope they know they could tell me anything and I would never judge them. I would do everything possible to show them the right direction to go and I would move mountains to keep them safe. They are my light. I know my husband; John feels the same way about the kids. He has kept me grounded also.

I get through each day for them. Some days I want to give up, although I will continue and with a smile on my face. I may be smiling but inside I am probably crying. I worry will I be alone when my time comes up. I do not want to be alone. I have even told my husband he is not allowed to go before me. I have had dreams where he is gone, and I am alone. I wake up tired and frustrated. I have never been afraid to be alone, but I do not want to be alone. It causes too much pain. You push away those who love you to keep them from having to deal with the pain inside yourself.

Do not get me wrong, my husband and I are with each other every minute we get. We have a silence that is comfortable. Mind you he has started to lose his hearing, so it is hard to communicate some days. I repeat myself so much I just do not say anything. And it is not his fault. He cannot help not being able to hear. I hate this as he was such a wonderful listener, and he also is an amazing guitarist. He has written as many songs as me and he loves the time he spends with the guys in his band. He is contemplating giving up, but I keep encouraging him to stay with it regardless of hearing. He can play by memory. He does find it difficult to play new stuff but there is a way. I keep hoping he finds a solution through the audiologists that will enable him to hear better. I laugh sometimes because he hears me when I swear at him. It is not often but he does.

Okay I give, you win
You're making my head spin.
Step up from there
Lead me anywhere.
Take my hand; hold tight.
Your love is out of sight.
Could you be for real?
Do I believe your spiel?
Wrap me up, lay me down
Be noisy: don't make a sound.
My heart is now yours
The blood in my head roars
Okay I'm yours; I submit
I was all along I admit.

KAL 05/14/97

Many times, I dream of being alone. Gone are my loved ones and I am sitting alone, tired and confused. I search where I am and cannot find them. I know they exist, and my heart is crushed because I cannot see them. The dream finds me in a place unfamiliar to me and the people I do see I do not recognize though they seem to know me. It is not a good dream. It is a nightmare and I rush to wake myself up because I do not like it. I sit up in my bed and I cannot get my breath. I feel like I have just run a marathon and it frightens myself.

I do not know if my dream is telling me to change and include others into what I feel inside or if it is showing me a life path I did not choose. I do not stay in the dream long enough to find out. I just want to wake up. The loneliness I feel inside tells me I do not want to know that truth. I recall so many lonely dreams I have had over the years. To me they are flashes of the path not chosen. What if I had married my high school love? What if I had not met my children's father? What if my loving husband today had not come into my life when he did? So many what ifs! I am afraid of never knowing my children on the different path. I am devastated without my husband, John. All these things fly around in my brain when I have those dreams. I must keep this reality and make the best of it. I need to deal with my innermost thoughts. I must release them into the universe and know I can exist without those truths. I can change any lies I have about myself if I just do it! I can do it! I will do it! I do not want my past marriage woes to creep into my marriage now. I have to stop being lonely, so I am not alone.

I'M NOT ALONE

I'm not alone
    I'm just lonely
I'm not happy
    Why can't you see?
      It's not easy to admit
    It wasn't in your kiss.
      I found out way too late
    It wasn't you I missed.
I'm not alone
    I'm just lonely

I'm not crying
    Maybe it's rain
Life is crazy
    Nothing is the same.
      Somehow, we fell apart
    We lost it somewhere
      The love isn't in your eyes
    But what do we care?
I'm not crying
    Maybe it's rain

I'm not staying
    I can't take anymore

I'm not leaving
    Through the front door
        One day we'll realize
    What it was that went wrong
        And we'll hear all about it
    In a "I'm gone" song
I'm not staying
    I can't take anymore.......

KAL 96/02/27

Is it a breakthrough? Am I going to be, okay? Will I continue forward and replace those dreams with my reality and be okay with it all? Can others still love me when I change? Should I change? When will I know I have changed? All these thoughts exploding at the same time. It is hard to keep up with them.

I know of one time in my life where I should have not made it home. I had just met Jay, but I also had accepted to go to a dance with a boy that rode my bus for school. So, it must have been late fall 1978. His name was Jack and I had told him I would go before I met Jay. Even though I had only met Jay I felt close to him. I went with Jack to the dance. He cheaped out and brought a Mickie so he would get pop free and add his own. I drank only pop as he never offered any to me. Actually, what he said was I should have brought my own. It was a nice dance with great music, but Jack did not dance. I had a few dances with the other girl sitting with us and one with a friend that was there also. After the dance I knew Jack was going to expect payment for taking me to the dance. On the way home, he turned down the back road that he lived on and once past all the farms, he pulled over and demanded sex. I told him no as this was just a first date, and I felt the date was more 'not a date' and besides I had met a young man the weekend before and wanted to explore that. He grabbed me and slapped me then went to punch me in the face, but I pulled away and he only hit my arm. He looked like a monster, and I was going to have to think quick to get out of this jam. I went for the door handle, and he yanked me back by my hair. I had flashbacks and the face I was seeing was that of my 'shadow'. I quickly thought how to get out of here. I panicked and searched for a little but strength and prayed. God came through.

While I was thinking he was yelling and had his hand around my throat. He told me 'I could kill you right here and right now. I could rape you before or after then dump your body out and no one would know it was me.' I took a breath and said everyone knows I was at the dance with you. He came back with he would tell everyone that we had a fight in the parking lot. I remembered waving at a friend as I got in the car. So, mentioned that would not be believable with her seeing me in the car. He said he would just say that I jumped out of the car because we were fighting in the car while driving home. I knew this would work for him to do but I told him my brothers and all their friends would never believe that and they would hunt him down like a dog and kill him if he laid one more hand on me. He thought about it and put the car in drive. I hugged the door and the handle and decided if he tried anything before, we got to my house I would jump out. He drove into our driveway, and I warned him that if he did not drive out sensibly, I would tell my brother's what he tried and then he could feel the way I just had. I slammed the door and ran into the house. I sat in my room at my window crying most of the night. My sister-in-law, Kim, had heard me crying and was going to come in but decided I just needed to be alone.

Honestly, I would have loved someone to hold me right about then. I never told anyone about that night. I knew if I told and my brother heard, he would have gone after him as he considered him a friend. I always wondered if he had done anything to anyone else. About a year later I heard he was getting married to a girl just turned sixteen. I figured he probably had raped her, and her parents made the wedding happen. I know they are not together now, but I felt for the girl. I know I should have spoken up now, but I was so scared if I spoke up and then talked to anyone my shadow may be discussed and I would lose Jay also. I just felt that Jay was someone I needed to know. After all he gave me four of the most wonderful children. Many times, through my life I felt God near me at needed events.

Life isn't supposed to drain you dry
   It isn't supposed to make you sad and cry
Life is supposed to bring you lots of love
   It was given to us from God up above.

Lately it feels like there is nowhere to go
   My heart is aching, and I feel so low

Where there was once joy, now replaced with sad.
 The life I cherished is only what I had.

I'm losing ground Lord and feel so lost
 I'm trying to get better at all costs
I need some guidance; please show the way
 Stay with me by my side each and every day.

My path was rocky, and I lost my plan
 Helping others; loving them and doing the best I can.
I now stand alone and look to You in the sky
 I need to know where I went wrong and why.

Lord, please be with me from this day forth.
 Help me determine my path and set me north
I need Your guidance, Your love and Your time
 To determine my future and show me what is mine.

KAL 17/08/01

Growing up in a big, noisy, and loving family was wonderful. Having many cousins always around kept our farms bustling. My mom was a saint. She worked from morning until night and never complained. She wrote in her diary every night, and she said nightly prayers for everyone. New people in our lives loved her. She was exceptional. She even was Citizen of the Year in the 90's. It was around 1990 or 1991. We all bought tickets to be there when she was presented, and she had no idea why their trip was rescheduled. Everyone kept the secret, and she was so beautiful that night. I always felt thankful for having her as my mom. She knew me, and I knew her heart.

My mom is one of the reasons I had to break free from the marriage. She was hurting with the pain I was feeling, knowing that my marriage had ended at some point, and I had to move to keep from losing myself completely. She did not want me to go west with Steve, and like I have said, she had asked John to intervene and convince me to stay in Ontario. He did try and in doing so I felt such a bond with him for being so nice to me. And life is funny as he dropped everything, including his job, and came west with me. My mom was more relieved that I had him in my corner. She even wrote him a beautiful letter knowing he would make sure no harm came to me.

I could not make it to my mom's funeral, but she knew I loved her. We did not need to be in the same room, house, city, or province to know how much. Besides, I did what my mom wanted. I stayed with my daughters and family to take care of their loss. That is what she wanted, and I did what she said. People were mad thinking I did not go but what they do not know is what she wanted. Besides, I was not allowed to travel outside of BC at that moment. You know Camp Cupcake and all and early parole with conditions.

I have told my son that is in Ontario the same thing. He knows I love him and when I die, I will see him and his family in Ontario. I will not be here any longer.

JUST A REFLECTION AWAY

I just looked in the mirror
    And suddenly I realized
        The reflection staring back at me
            Was as if it was my mother's eyes.

I don't know when it was
    That my mother became me
        But it did happen, though
            That is plain to see.

It is now I realize
    Just how my mother felt
        And thinking of that feeling
            Makes my heart melt.

For now, I understand
    Everything I put her through
        If I could start all over
            There's so much I could do.

I'd tell her I love her more
    And appreciate her thoughts
        Even just a simple hug
            Would surely mean a lot.

Now that I'm all grown up
    And our busy lives keep us apart
        It's nice to know I've got a piece
            Of my mother spreading out from my heart.

I don't mind seeing my mother
    In my mirror each passing day
        Because when I'm not near her
            She's just a reflection away.

TOBY

I tried to model my parenting to my mom's, but I am sure I fell short of her example. I did not have the same patience as she did. But I tried. I am sure my oldest endured the most of my learning to be a mom. And I was not as happy then as I am today. I still was carrying my 'shadow' around and sleep was elusive to me. It is not a good steppingstone, but as I dealt with my demons, I became a better mom. My mom was with me a lot and she did rub off. When I moved, besides my kids, she was the one I missed the most. But over the miles we connected better as we could talk about almost anything.

I worried about her aging, but mom had my sisters and sister in laws to tend and visit her. My mom was priceless when she called. I would answer the phone and we would share any news we had and talk about the weather. Near the end of the call she would say, 'Well thanks for calling and be gone.' Just like when her mom would call her and do the same and my mom would look at the phone back then and say I guess gramma was done talking. So funny. I would do the same when she started doing that.

Mom had a lot of knowledge and was one of the smartest women I knew. Dad was smart but he was not allowed to finish school. Mom graduated from high school and dad had to leave after the eight grades to take care of the farm. My gramps was unable to manage with his hernia…. well, he could have but he was stubborn, and I believe he liked being the overseer instead of the working man.

Mom and dad were the hardest working people I knew. Worked the farm, worked off the farm, did volunteer work, managed all us children and everyone else's also and still had time to relax and do things they wanted to do. I always imagined them finally getting old enough to sit back and relax together. God had other plans and dad died before they could. Although I am sure they would have still been as busy as they were in their younger years.

God has them in Heaven and I feel their presence every day. I even talk to them as much as I pray to God. I have always felt my Gramma Mabel in my life since she passed when I was so young. So now I have all my ancestors watching over me including my loving sister, Colleen.

OH MOM, CAN YOU SEE?

Oh mom, can you see what it is that I am?
Oh mom, can you see what it is that I am?
I'll be what I'll be, I'll do what I'll do.
Oh mom, can you see I'm just like you?

> You taught me how to be a good wife
> Just by the way you loved my dad.
> You showed me how to do the best
> With anything that I had.

Oh mom, can you see what it is that I am?
Oh mom, can you see what it is that I am?
I'll be what I'll be, I'll do what I'll do.
Oh mom, can you see I'm just like you?

> I try so hard to be very good.
> And show my children my love.
> You taught me to pray and to give thanks
> And believe in our God up above.

Oh mom, can you see what it is that I am?
Oh mom, can you see what it is that I am?
I'll be what I'll be, I'll do what I'll do.
Oh mom, can you see I'm just like you?

> I hope and I pray that you'll finally see
> I've tried to be there for you
> And when times are tough, it's you I think of
> You're smiling face pulls me through.

Oh mom, can you see what it is that I am?
Oh mom, can you see what it is that I am?
I'll be what I'll be, I'll do what I'll do.
Oh mom, can you see I'm just like you?

Oh mom, can you see what it is that I am?
Oh mom, can you see what it is that I am?
I'll be what I'll be, I'll do what I'll do.
Oh mom, can you see I'm just like you?

TOBY

When Colleen passed and Mom the next year, I rewrote one of the poems/songs I started, and it stands for my Mom and my sister.

MAMA'S GOING TO CANDY HEAVEN

Mama's going to Candy Heaven
At least that's what she told me today
She cried as she said she doesn't want to go
But God needs her to come right away.

He needs her to make her sweet candy
Up in Heaven for all of His people there.
And the sooner she can come the better
And she'd make lots so they can share.

Mama's going to Candy Heaven
At least that's what she told me today
She cried as she said she doesn't want to go
But God needs her to come right away.

And she promised she'd make me more candy
She'd show me how to make it just like her.
So, one day I could come to Candy Heaven
And again, we could finally be close and near.

Mama's going to Candy Heaven
At least that's what she told me today
She cried as she said she doesn't want to go
But God needs her to come right away.

Mama's going to Candy Heaven
And God needs her to come right away
Mama's gone to Candy Heaven
We buried her today....

KAL 17/04/16

Colleen passed too soon. She was a rock for her family and for all. She was like my mom in many ways. Elizabeth is still alive, and I think she has my gramma Mabel's traits which I love. We are close but I wish closer. I am sure if we were closer and talked more, we would discuss our 'shadow'. That would help heal both our spirits. Although I think Elizabeth handled her own battle very well. She is a well-balanced woman and has a wonderful supportive husband. I miss my sister, Colleen, a lot. She was taken way too soon from us. We were supposed to have our twilight years to sit and reminisce. Elizabeth and I will have to do that, and I am sure Colleen will be listening. She is one of our angels.

I asked God to let me know
If you were okay today.
I prayed that He would tell
Me somehow and some way.
We pray for many things
Every night and every day
Just let me know that
All is well, my angel is okay.
And I listened and looked
To see if He answered me
A little bird hops on the ground
I'm sure I felt you near me
My faith is strong Lord
I believe that was my sign.
I thank You for Your love
As always angel of mine.

KAL 17/05/31

Colleen was so musical. She could sing, she could pick up a tune on the piano and played guitar. Her second husband taught her guitar, and her last husband was also a guitar player and loved to sing with her.

She played a new tune as she strummed her guitar
Then looked around and noticed she was not alone
It pleased her to know they'd come to hear her play
She gave them the best they'd ever known

Her voice was strong as her foot tapped along
Every knew she gave her all in her songs
They all listened and danced as she gave it her all
She yodelled and she smiled, and she stood tall

When God came calling, she tried her very best
To stay a little longer and keep singing her songs
But time came to pass, and God called her home
We didn't want to let go but he needed her to come along

Her voice was strong as her foot tapped along
Every knew she gave her all in her songs
They all listened and danced as she gave it her all
She yodelled and she smiled, and she stood tall

Life continues on and we miss her dearly you know
She sings in God's choir and He's happy too
My sister is an angel and watches over us all
In our hearts she's still here and it will have to do.

Her voice was strong as her foot tapped along
Every knew she gave her all in her songs
They all listened and danced as she gave it her all
She yodelled and she smiled, and she stood tall

KAL *17/05/04*

As I grew up and had my family, I started immersing myself into being busy all the time. Something like my mom, but I went overboard. I was so busy I never took care of myself. Seeing other people happy made more sense to me. The one thing I enjoyed the most was baseball. I had played when I was younger so coaching my kid's teams just felt right. That would be okay if that were all I did. I coached one team to begin with. Then I added on another the next year. Before I knew it, I was coaching or at least assistant coach for five teams. My oldest, Jaymee played on three teams. I coached one, I assisted the next and I went and watched the third. My oldest daughter, Kayla, played on two teams. I coached one and assisted the other. Then there was my youngest two where I assisted their team. Thank God they were on the same team most of the time. I was also president of the Richmond Minor Ball League and the secretary of the Tri-County Minor Ball League. At the same time, I was working full time, Pathfinder and Girl Guide leader and Co-Leader of Sparks.

My ex had started pulling away from the kids and me. He worked fulltime afternoons. He got up with the kids and made sure they got on the bus and took care of the ones not in school until he needed to get ready to work. My mom and my niece took over the kids until I came home from work around 5:30pm and I took over. I had laundry to do, housecleaning, and do all the running around for whatever the kids were into. I stayed up until Jay came home at 1am because he said he hated coming home to any empty house. Once he was home, I would try to get some sleep until I got up at 6am to go to work. The weekends were hectic, and Jay and I had decided that Saturdays I would sleep in, and Sundays was his day. Well, that did not work as from the time the kids got up on Saturday's he would be yelling at them to be quiet, or they would wake me up. I was awake anyhow listening to him yell. Sunday's, he loved it, the kids and I got up, got dressed, and headed to church so the house was quiet as a church mouse until we came home at noon. I loved going to church and Sunday school with my mom and kids. Most of the family went and after everyone came back to the farmhouse for the day.

Even when we did not live on the farm, we came to my parent's every weekend. It soothed my soul to be near them and to attend church with my mom. My dad went but not all the time. And after he passed mom needed us to be there with her. My life was busy enough that I did not feel the shadow as much. I created my Heaven and pushed away Hell. But I knew it would rear itself and I prepared for that. I usually did not let anyone know when it did. I kept it bottled in. Once we lived back at the farmhouse, I knew I would have to deal with it at some point. I thought my marriage was doing well until my dad took sick and Jay started pulling away from being part of anything. He had his own demons, I had mine. I had to wait to deal with mine, but once it started up, I too pulled away. We were both hurting, but not together. I asked Jay when I told him I had to move away to come with me and keep our family together. He was not ready to do that. He absolutely hated change. I had to leave or risk not being alive. The shadow was looming, and I had to get away from it. So, I chose to go without him. I wish we could have known how each other felt without all the baggage we were carrying.

In the end, it was for the best. I had met John; he was making sure I got to BC safely and out of that friendship grew love. A love I was not looking for, but desperately needed. And I believe a love for which I was waiting.

Standing, yes, I am standing
    Alive, yet feeling a lot of dread
Moving, I think forward
    Thoughts spinning in my head

Calm myself slowly, gently
    Lay down my strife and see
What it is I need to do
    Who it is that I should be?

Turning another chapter in life
    Striving to be the best of me
Reaching out my heart and hand
    That others will this truly see

Wanting to make others happy
    Their trust working to get back
It will be hard I knew this
    With so much against me stacked

Proving myself will be my goal
    Standing straight and surely
One foot in front of the other
    I wait and will wait patiently.

KAL 17/09/19

I am always waiting in my life. I spend hours sitting in my van waiting to pick up and drop off family and friends. It is nothing new to wait. As a child I would wait in the vehicle with my mom when my dad would stop for just a minute to talk to another farmer. Thirty minutes later he might be out to leave. Getting rides to baseball games could take forever. I can remember sitting at the window (yes, I know a watch pot never boils) and willing Dad to drive up the eighth (concession by the farm leading to hwy #3, which turned into the seventh over the years) and be home to take me to wherever I was due to go.

I wait for everything in my life.
It's the way it has always been
Although I try to make things right
I fail so often that is how it seems
I wish I could go back again
To change outcomes, that's a dream.
 I have tried so hard all by myself
 To please everyone through the years
 I show my smiles and comfort many
 Then behind closed doors I shed my tears
 It seems like no matter how hard I try
 Some are not grateful; some are, and I hold them dear.
When I see good results, I feel well
And glad that I helped them all out
I still would try to do my very best
No matter what the problem was about
I have a hard time not to get involved
To comfort their fears; take away all doubt
 I'm trying to hold back; stay away
 But when they need me, I turn to them
 I'll wipe tears, I'll comfort, I'll help
 And also, all my love I would send
 Though I can't give more than I have
 I'll do what I can and give what I can lend.

KAL 17/06/02

Writing is liberating and helps to form better ideas. It clears the mind and I have used writing as a method to unmuddle my thoughts. Many times, I sit down knowing I needed to express my feelings and before I realize, it is hours later, and I have not yet written anything. Confusing for sure. Then other times I do not intend to write, and I pump out page after page. Whether it is a song, a poem, or part of a book.

It's no use, you know, right now
    I cannot find any words.
What use to flow so freely,
    Cannot even slightly be heard.

They have disappeared again
    And I know not where they go.
But just as quick as they left
    They're back again, you know.

Sometimes it will happen
    When you least expect it to.
My mouth will be wide open
    But no sounds are coming through.

Or right in the middle of writing
    The pen just seems to drop.
The words are stuck inside it
    And my fingers have all but stopped

And try as I might to find them,
    They are mysteriously gone.
And just as quickly as they left
    They'll come back one by one.

So please will you excuse me
    If I do seem all confused.
Maybe my words do fail me
    Because they've all been used?

TOBY

I wish I could just explain my life and fix all the blunders and misconceptions. That would be too easy though. What holds me back is quite common. Would anyone want to read what I write? Will I be judged opposite of what I am trying to say? Can anyone understand the jumble of words and thoughts? Should I write about everything, especially the bad? Did I write it down in proper speak, or in proper order? Do I give explicit details? Why am I hesitant? Is this normal to feel this way? So many questions, so many words, so many directions, so many truths to uncover the lies. Its hard, you know. That shadow looms on the wall sometimes and I do not even see it. But it shows in what I am writing now.

Life's too short to worry about tomorrow
Worrying too much only brings sorrow
God has planned our lives before we were born.
Sleep well each night and smile each morn.

Everything that happens is part of a master plan.
Keep your chin up high and take a firm stand.
Behind each of us there is an endless love
From all around us and from above.

When tomorrow comes, face it with a smile
For God is with you every little mile.
And besides this bountiful feeling from above
Are my thoughts, my prayers and all my love.

TOBY

I sincerely wish I could talk to my sister Beth about all this. She took university classes that maybe helped her. But maybe she has suppressed all those thoughts and what happened years ago, and it would be too painful for her to talk about it again. The little bits of information I have told doctors is not enough for them to see how it affects me. The one doctor I saw in Calgary pinpointed a little bit, but I was evasive and did not tell him more than he asked for. See that is how those appointments go. I do not think an hour in a room with someone you have never met can release the pain inside. I, often, feel like I am a child and want to sit in a ball on the floor, but I do not. I want to scream at the top of my lungs what happened to me. Every little thing in my life that happened and even what I did that was wrong. To make sense of action and reaction would be comforting, I think. To make sense of the wrongs I did after dealing with the wrongs against me.

Many words, many phrases
    Are deep within my mind.
I'm sure I'll use each
    Of them over my lifetime.
I've not said all I can
    To everyone I do know.
Some will be amazed
    That I can love them so.
I am not ready to stay quiet
    And keep my thoughts inside.
Some people are content as such
    But not me – my feelings never hide.
So please forgive me if at
    Some time I do forget to say,
All the words inside me
    That should come your way.
Or if I say too much
    And you are sure I've lost it,
It's just my inner self
    In all its glory and wit
Telling you I care deeply
    And will always be the one
To tell you quite honestly
    My words, my phrases will never be done.

KAL 03/21/96

I know God had a plan, but I believe circumstances led me away from that plan. Does not mean I do not reach out to help others. That is something instilled within my soul.

My life was planned for me from the start.
    I was born on time with a strong healthy heart.
I had a great life and think I always knew
    What it was God had sent me to do.

I took my time to learn about life.
    What it was all about and each man's plight.
Unfortunately, somewhere I lost my way
    I went off course and forgot to pray.

Almost too late a person changes step
    Reaches down inside into their inner depths.
And God is good and a sympathetic God.
    He forgives and on with life we plod.

I was put here to enjoy and love
    All that's within and around me and above.
To make each person I come in contact with
    Forget their woes and their spirit lift.

And once I've accomplished all of this
    I'll take some time and make sure I didn't miss
Anyone who needed me to be their friend.
    For this is the main reason God did me send.

So, when my time on earth is near done
    My friends will remember and to me will come.
To hug and laugh, to kiss and cry, to help me
    Hold up my head and not ask me why.

I knew God was right to make me live
    My life to the fullest and a purpose give.
No matter how long I'm here I'll give my best.
    Live for each day, give my all no less.

TOBY

Saying I was a good girl when young would not be the truth. When I would do something out of character, instead of trying to figure out why, I would be punished. Many times, I was sent to my room for speaking out or lashing out at a sibling. I wanted justification for everything, and I challenged my parents on many points. I am sure they worried for me, but not knowing anything is wrong inside they were not prepared for digging deeper. I know I should have told them when everything happened, but as years come and go, it buries deeper.

I am enormously proud of my oldest daughter, Kayla, she went through nine years of hell and stepped out of it and told what was going on behind closed doors. I think about the few times she would ask a strange question or say something I should have perked up and asked for more info. Such is, "mom, you don't know what he says and does to me" or "did you read my one poem? What did you think?" It is times I should have said tell me more please, but I did not and that upsets me. I am at fault for not hearing what she was really saying. I did not want to deal with something that I was not sure how. I just was so glad she was stronger than I ever was and spoke out to silence the pain she had been enduring. She will live with that all her life also, but she was brave enough to do something about it. This will make her children stronger in the end also. She knew enough to get help and I thank God and the people she reached out to for that.

That is her story to tell, and I am only support. I do know how excited and how relaxed my grandchildren and Kayla became when he was found guilty and sentenced. They started to live finally. Now he had been granted an appeal based on the wording used by the judge and one of the questions from crown being improperly said or written. How foolish is the justice system? Now they must endure the whole court proceedings all over again. She has now to relive the events as she tells the court. How unfair this all is, and I know it will affect them again. It pisses one off when that happens. Why cannot victims be left in peace. He is so narcissistic, and this is just another ploy to make her uncomfortable and anxious again. The peace they had found is disrupted. Kayla must relive all the trauma on the stand again, Josh must tell his story again to the court system. I must tell what I knew, although Kayla protected even me from knowing the worst of it. Why is it that the victim suffers over and over and then the court system allows them to be badgered by defence lawyers? It just is not right at all and must be overhauled. The narcissist should not be able to gloat over their control of the victim. It just is not right.

PEACE

Noises coming from everywhere,
   Crashing, banging, booming.
     I look here, I look there.
   Somehow, I will find the peace.
that everyone so earnestly searches for.

Silence in but a golden word
   that only is found across the way.
     Never peaceful is our lives.
   The whole world's running over-time.
Let me out to find my peace.

Crash, boom, clatter, bang.
   This is your life, not to be mine.
     Where I'm going is across the way.
   I'll find silence when I reach
My ultimate dream --- PEACE.

TOBY

I feel the pain also as I know how I have felt, and their lives were so much more filled with abuse and for a much longer time. My pain is minimal reliving what I held in for so long. I think that is why I just figured I was lucky and had buried it all so far down. I had painted over the shadow on the wall, and yet there it is when I least expect it. I can only pray that my daughters and children do not have to suppress themselves and get all the help available to them nowadays.

Dealing with life is hard enough without any trauma. I sit and listen to others whenever I can. It could be in a bunch of people at a house party, a dance, at the park, just walking in the mall or down the street. I see trauma happening sometimes, but I am afraid to say much to strangers. What I do is make myself seen and usually the trauma goes away. What I mean is at the park a mother is chastising their child for getting dirty on the playground, so I move closer, and I talk to my grandkids telling them to have a blast, get dirty, enjoy your play, and do not worry about a thing in the world. The mother quite often will stop and listen and realize they are being an overbearing, stressful person. Now that child can play like a child should – without a care in

the world except to have fun. You get a peaceful quiet feeling inside
knowing you helped in just a little way.

The sunshine is warm upon my face
And I bow my head to say God's grace
As I speak and ask to be in His favour
I wish for forgiveness and even more

The birds fly above and sing their songs
I think of my family and all that I long
I try to remember that God is with me always
Every night that I sleep and wake to the day

When you look around and see others' smiles
You think of loved ones across many miles
The clouds look like familiar faces or loved pets
And still there is more as God's not done yet

I know God forgives us our sins as we pray
He is always listening to all of us every day
So, when a butterfly lands on my hand or finger
I'll know He is talking to me and let it linger

No longer the darkness of night will I fear
And it's okay on days when I'm sad or tear
I trust that God will continue to guide my way
I pray for His forgiveness and His love everyday

KAL 17/06/06

At night my mind tries to settle and I really try to think of something happy before I fall asleep. But many nights my pleasant thoughts become overshadowed by the shadow on the wall. I get angry with myself when I wake and shake off those feelings and try to start a new happy dream. It works sometimes, but now always. I am tired myself of waking more tired than I went to sleep. I imagine how my daughter feels and I pray she has methods of removing the trauma she has been through. God I pray hard for that.

Quiet, so quiet, dark and gloomy
Quiet, so quiet, dark and gloomy

    Hurting all over, pain has increased
    Hurting all over, pain has increased

Crying again, now what is wrong?
Crying again, now what is wrong?

    Tears fall freely, down my cheeks
    Tears fall freely, down my cheeks

Am I coping, am I okay?
Am I coping, am I okay?

Quiet, so quiet, dark and gloomy
Quiet, so quiet, dark and gloomy

KAL 17/04/27

Jumping back to some of my feelings in life. They come and go; they are up then down; happy then sad; elated then remorseful; satisfied then unsure. It is a big world out there. I get so weighed down feeling those around me and their troubles.

I have a feeling of desolation
    It creeps upon me all at once
I can't control it when it comes
    The days turn into weeks and months

I try to not think about it
    But it worms its way into my heart

Then makes me feel I'm in a rainstorm
    All alone and the tears begin to start

I sob quietly into my pillows
    I cover my head and just let it go
This feeling takes me on a journey
    Where I am I do not know

I try so hard to keep on smiling
    And to be pleasant to everybody
I hide my sorrow and keep it inside
    They only see the happy side of me.

KAL 17/04/26

I take a lot of care to move forward. I try to listen to others without judgement. I cannot rationalize some people and I can be standing right there and not hear a single word for some reason. I wish I could help everyone I meet. I feel for anyone having a bad day. When I see someone on the street homeless it pains me to not be able to help more. Lack of funds restricts me from helping monetarily but I have smiles, a listening ear and time to give. It is hard to know whether you should approach or not, but for the most they all just want to talk to someone.

The clock ticks on and yet stands still
I stand here and wait for the unknown
Looking around everyone else moves about
Faces all around me yet here I am alone

The sun shines down, and I can't see ahead
I know where I was but now, I'm not sure
It is supposed to be warm yet I shiver inside
I'm searching; I don't know what I'm here for

The birds must be chirping, though I hear nothing
I struggle to listen, and still I'm missing the sound
Where did my life go, I must find it again!
Where once there was joy, now feelings are down.

As the day turns to night, I can find nobody
I am still alone staying inside my head
They all talk around me, and I want to belong
If only I could concentrate on what is said.

Now it is nighttime and I feel still confused
The day came and went without me again
Others have changed also; I see it too
But I feel the same, the tears fall like rain.

KAL 17/09/09

I float through each day and make grand plans to be productive. In
my mind I formulate exactly what I should do. In my heart I know it
is a good plan. In reality, I struggle to get anything done. It took me 3
weeks to finally shake out all the rugs, wash the floors and vacuum
throughout our tiny space. I guess I should be elated that I completed
it at all. I have trouble admitting that having fibromyalgia and
Raynaud's affects my daily life, but it does. Anyone that has been
diagnosed with fibromyalgia knows it is not a disease that is not
forgiving. I try not to dwell on what I cannot do and think of things I
can do. Each day is a whole new ball game. Most days I wake so tired
I think I should just go back to bed, but experience has told me (as
well as my mom) to get on with the day and sleep at night. Usually
this is true for me. Lately though I feel so numb from pain, tired
from lack of sleep and moody. I try so hard for others not to see any
of this, but it sneaks through some times. The pain from fibromyalgia
is sometimes so intense you want to scream, yet some days you find a
smidgeon of energy and go like heck until it runs out and your body
tells you that you will pay for that later when you try and sleep. I can
have pain in so many places of my body I cannot tell where it hurts
the most. The headaches were the telling sign for me. I used to have
so many headaches I could not tell when one ended and another
began. Once my medication has been figured out the headaches
lessened. Saying I feel great is an exaggeration. Do I feel good some
days? Yes, I can say that.

My doctors told me that fibromyalgia is usually brought on by
something tragic happening in your life or an accident. Now they are
ruling some of the preconceived notions out. I wonder if for me it
could trace back to when I was a child. Was the trauma of being *raped*

in my youth what caused my body to slowly get to a point that it screamed out also? I used to think it was my dad being diagnosed with brain tumours that was the beginning, but now I feel I have had it longer. I imagine as with the scared little girl within, she tried to get through to me by creating my poetry and songs. Yes, they helped although I think my fibromyalgia is in a way her screaming for relief and to be healed. The medication helps me help her. Sounds weird, but who knows. I am sure if I ever found a person, I could talk to about this and feel they were helping, maybe, just maybe I could figure it all out.

I feel lost and like I am searching for something. It seems when I get close to whatever it is I get lost yet again. It is like chasing a leaf down a stream, just when you get close you lose sight of it. You see it again and try to follow it. Some days I wish I were that leaf and could just float down the stream.

The water trickles on
from where it came before.
I can hear it calling
out to listen for just a while.
But for many small reasons.
there isn't time to hear
the story it could tell me
as it had journeyed each mile.
The stream becomes a river
and so, it carries further on.
I can hear it calling
out to sit and enjoy it's beauty.
But for some more reasons
there isn't time to watch
the beauty of the river
as it headed for the sea.
The ocean is so vast
that it can take your breath away.
I can hear it calling
out to relax and walk its shores.
But for unknown reasons
there isn't time to walk
the ocean's shores so smooth
as it ripples ever more.
The tear trickles down

my cheek and onto my heart
I can hear it calling
out to care before it's too late.
But for no more reasons
there is not time to care.
The tear brings back memories
as it for a smile now waits.

KAL 05/12/96

Throughout life I have always felt there was someone close to me when I was at my worst. I felt it was a loved family member that had gone to Heaven. Sometimes it felt different, so I decided that it was not always the same one. My gramma on my dad's side was close to me and I felt she was with me on many occasions. There were times I was sure I could sense one of my gramps or my dad. They were there on some of the more dangerous times in my life. And yet there were times as a young woman I just knew my gramma on my mom's side was there. My sister passed just before I went to Camp Cupcake, and I felt her there many nights. Lately it has been my mom and my friend, Chris that visits. It is comforting to feel they are around still.

THANK YOU GUIDING STARS

There are times in one's life that you fall down and cry.
You are not proud, but still alive, asking yourself and others why!
Once you've accepted your fate and ask God to forgive all
You may need a helping hand, yet not know who to call.

The road home will be bumpy; you will falter but trudge on
There are angels watching over you, they were there all along.
You are on your way, though struggling, friendship is offered to you.
Take that hand and stand up, they are there to help you through.

Thank you to each and everyone, along the difficult way home
They have given you a new chance to prove yourself, you know.
There are not enough words to tell how special they are.
They stay within your heart always to be one of your guiding stars.

KAL 17/09/28

When my first marriage started to fall apart, I went through tremendous changes. I tried so valiantly to hold the family together. My first husband just did not want to work on our relationship. He never has liked any kind of problem solving. He would rather shy away and not think about any of it. So slowly I was getting confused, feeling more alone, losing a lot of weight, and making many decisions that should have been between Jay and myself. I cannot say I hate my first husband, but I started to feel like I was his mother. I just fell out love with him. I care how he is, but he has a new wife, and she has fallen into being his mom too. I hear from the kids once in awhile about how he is doing. If we are in the same place, we are cordial. I am happy that he has moved on and did not fall into a gutter somewhere as he very well could have. His family was not a good example of how to live, that is for sure.

They say I'm all confused.
    I don't know which end is up.
You know they may be right
    Cause I've had nothing but bad luck.
Could I possibly be wrong?
    And now I'm back on track?
Or am I just hiding away,
    So, is it confidence I lack?
Each day that has come along
    I lose track of yet another thing.
I start to flounder away
    Then I'm back and I could sing.
No, I'm not confused really
    Just caught in a revolving door.
Soon I'll have to stop whirling,
    Cause I just can't take any more.

KAL(TOBY) 02/27/96

Along with poetry I write songs, well folk songs mostly like my gramps. It comes flowing out. First, it is a poem, then suddenly it is a song. Most I have put to music within my own means. That is me and my tape recorder at first, then me and my computer. I love seeing the result. Some are sappy love songs, some are straight up folk songs, some are 'churchy' as my grandkids would say and a few kinds of dark. This is the first one I am including with poetry. It was a poem until I looked at it and realized it should be a hymn.

There is a flower growing in this garden
It blooms so brightly; makes us smile
Makes us glad to know that God is with us
No matter how life is sad once in a while.
> *C: There is a church down on the corner*
> *That gives us faith in our Lord above*
> *It helps our faith and teaches others*
> *God cares for all, and we are loved*

There is a faith we all believe in
And it keeps us happy for all eternity
We are so fortunate to have our Saviour
He watches over us, cares so lovingly
C:
There is a cross; we all have seen it
High up on a hill but not alone
Our Saviour died there to save His flock
He gave us a better life than we would ever know

KAL 17/05/09

I can say without doubt that I have always floundered in life. I am
never quite certain if I say the right thing or step the right way. I
guess I was destined to fall more than once. I always wonder if I was
supposed to be born. I know many think about that occasionally. But
I think it so often. I think if had not been born then maybe my baby
brother would have lived. It is possible the shadow on the wall really
knew I was not supposed to be there. Is it thinkable that I was not
where I was supposed to be and lived past my expiry date? I think
these thoughts many times. Like I have said I do not consider myself
to be suicidal because I am such a wimp. I could never purposely
injure myself or anyone else. Even thinking these thoughts and
putting them in black and white is not something I would do. But
here we are….

I just now realized a big part of me has died,
And the life I have been leading is all a lie.
I don't belong where I am, doing the things I do.
It's time to move on, for that life is all through.
It came all of a sudden, it hit me really hard.
And the power of its impact has left a little scar.
I know not what it is that I really should begin.
I just know I can't continue from where I've been.
So, I'll start again fresh, as soon as I mend.
I don't know what I'll be, nor how or when.
To suddenly find you're not where you should be
Puts you back at a beginning, scared and lonely
But I have a feeling deep within my soul
That I can learn from mistakes and use what I know
Even though I can't decide what my new life will become
There's no turning back and away from it I can't run

TOBY

Living with constant pain numbs you to a point that you know you
still are hurting but it does not let up. When someone asks how you
are, you reply okay because it is still the same as the day before. It will
be there tonight, tomorrow and the next. Yes, my doctors have tried
many medications. Some have worked, most have not. The next thing
that upsets your daily meds is a shortage of the one that does the
most. I have a pain reliever that took many tries to get to that is
currently out of stock. I can coast for about a month, but it has been

almost three months with another three at the earliest. This should not happen in today's times. But that would be a result of Covid-19. There I have put that down so will have to talk some about that later.

Regardless I am in pain. My doctor has prescribed two tries at something to help. The first I had a terrible reaction to and the second is okay, but I am not sleeping with that one. The pain has lessened but my body cries out for something more to work.

Deep down the
    abyss of the mountain
Far away from
    civilized thoughts.
I gaze through
    the settling mist
And know the
    being I'm not.
High above the
    snow capped mountain
Near the center
    of billowy cloud,
I peer through
    the dewy fog
And know not how
    much is allowed.
Way below the
    deep dark mountain
Close to the
    moss on the rock,
I see clearly
    through the night.
Somewhere over the
    side of the mountain,
Away from all
    who look to see,
I look through
    the wants of others
And know the
    person I must be.

Before the shadow came to be on my wall, I did have a great childhood. Being the youngest of seven had its merits and its downside also. Everyone that visited always made a fuss over me for the first few years. I did get away with no bedtime. I, also, had fun with all my siblings and cousins when we got together. I can remember hide and seek in the corn field. I will be honest and say I would not play it today. As a child there was no worries about what may be in the field with you that you could not see. I am sure there were wild animals in there that I did not come across. And the few times they forgot about me, and I had to try and find my way back to the pole light in the driveway. We were extremely excited when hydro came and put a dusk to dawn light a little closer to the far barn. It worked without having to turn it on – wow!

I spent more time riding around the driveway circle or in the hay barn talking to the dog. I would plan my plight in life or pretend to run away. My plight ended with an early death and how each family member would react. Running away was exciting in my head until I would realize no one even noticed when I was up in the barn for hours on end, just dreaming.

Wearily, trudging along the road
Step by step, bringing me closer to home.
Along the way I pass a child
Who has nothing to do but roam?

This makes me stop to think
I remember being like that child.
Today I go, I do, I return once more.
There is no free time – not even once in a while.

When I think of times when I was young
And roaming was all a part of my day.
I laughed more, danced more, and worked less.
I was more carefree to my parent's dismay.

I long for those days and all the memories
And I need to get back to a simpler time
So, like that child, I will try to relax more
Dance more, laugh always until the bells do chime.

I do wish I could just snap a finger and help everyone near me get through whatever it is that they are having troubles with. I worry about how others feel more than myself. I feel their angst and their worries. In the middle of a group of strangers I can feel their woes. And if I am not around anyone all my own insecurities come crashing down. It is like everything I have questioned in my life haunts me over and over. I, firmly, believe my life would have been a lot different if the shadow had never happened.

I wonder if it was the trauma of abuse that brought on my empathetic soul. It is like being empathetic drowns out my own pain. When I am busy helping others, my pain takes a backseat. As I have said before, my doctor told me that my fibromyalgia was brought on by something traumatic in my life. I used to think it was my dad becoming ill but talking to a specialist and recounting when it was that I could sleep well and did not have bad dreams that goes back to childhood. Go figure!

You will find that many teenagers think about death. Most envision their deaths. When I was a teenager suicide was not a massive thing. It happened but I have found as the years come and go, it increases. I thought about death. I dreamt of my death a thousand times, but at no time did I feel I would die at my own hands. I was ready as a teenager to accept if my time came up. Each year I thank God for one more year with my family. Now my feelings are the same except I do worry for my grandchildren. I see the world we live in and think what they will have when they grow old. I worry whether their parents will be able to help them. None the less I am ready. I have not finished with all I would like to, but I am ready.

WHAT IS DEATH?

What is death? A question often raised
Is it a time of grief and sorrow?
Where you believe in no tomorrow?

I've often wondered when I'm alone
If death is an end to life
Or is it a new beginning
Away from all this toil and strife?

Many people have different feelings
About death they won't discuss.
And when asked to explain it
They will raise a terrible fuss.

Myself, I'd like to believe
That death is the wrong word.
For when a person passes on
There should be rejoicing heard.

They have not really left themselves
Just moved on to start again
In another place of time.
Not death, but rebirth should be the name.

So, what is death? Again, the question raised.
It is not a time of grief and sorrow,
But a rebirthing to believe in tomorrow.

TOBY

I do not tell people I was in a troubled marriage the first time around.
We were very mismatched that is for sure. Jay was someone different.
We fell in love too quickly and he proposed after just a month of
seeing each other. Our wedding was June 15th, 1979. It was rocky for
the first few years as we learnt each other's natural tendencies. To be
honest I was not sure we would make it to 5 years. His family were
alcoholics and drug users. My mission was to love him until he knew
he did not have to be like them. He had slips but for the most part he
did well. Jay's family did not understand my family values also, so it
was back and forth. When Jay would be with his family or friends, I

had to keep a watchful eye to help him make better choices. I can say without a doubt I still love Jay but as I realized years ago, I loved him because he needed help. I was in love with helping him. He thinks he is not smart, but I see a wonderful father and grandfather that just needs to know with confidence he is enough!

WHAT TO DO?

I just don't know
What I'm going to do now.
Everything is so mixed up
Pour another drink; drain the cup.

Is that all there is to life?
I'd rather you just used the knife.
Things are getting out of hand
Either I change or find some other man.

I wouldn't want you to change
That would hurt your image.
I'll have to become more understanding
Would that mean anything?

I just don't understand or know
If the change will ever show?

TOBY

My dad passed away in 1992, that left a big hole in my life. It brought out the pain I have with fibromyalgia. It made me look at my own life in prospective of my marriage. I still loved Jay, but I realized it was not a strong love as when we first met. I was mothering him, and he was happy just existing and letting me do everything and direct what we did. I was sad. Our kids were the string holding us together. We did everything for them and not for ourselves. It was an ah-ha moment. It was then that I started watching what our homelife was like. I ached for someone to take control of me and let me relax finally. My mom did speak with Jay and tell him that he needed to step up and be a husband. He had to help me, or he would lose me. That did not happen. And slowly I was wasting away. I lost weight. I was not happy as I could be.

What happened next, I still think about. In 1994 there was an obituary of my long lost first love's mom. I reached out as a friend and sent condolences from Jay and myself. He responded quickly thanking me and we started writing each other. I kept it simple as a friend for the first few months. He had me realize that maintaining my marriage was not good for me or my kids. I started to morph out of my shell and be happier than I had been. Happier, yet more confused. I talked daily with another friend, Bob. He had helped me get through my dad's illness and death. Steve was a fall back to simpler days. He had been married once with no children of his own. He asked tough questions of me. I still have all the letters he wrote to me. Within two years of writing, I knew I had to get away from everything in my life before I fell into a pool of despair and quietly slip away from life itself. I look at a photo of myself in May of 1996, shortly after I moved away from home and there is nothing to me. The plan was for Steve to come west with me, but John changed that very quickly. I still love Steve also but that is a first love kind of feeling. John is true love. We were friends, we consoled each other, we fell in love, and we chose each other. He is a lasting love that I truly needed. It was a long road and here I am.

When the road seems so long
  and you feel like giving in,
Say a prayer, close your eyes
  and struggle on, hold on if you can.

Life sometimes has a way
  of tricking you into believing
You can't make it, but you can.
  The horizon is only deceiving.

The closer you seem to get
  to what it is you value most,
The harder the way may get.
  Life is hard, you cannot coast.

Keep on trudging even though
  the challenges will be hard.
If you just believe, it will happen
  it was all planned from the start.

And when you've made it there
  you must remember then
That someone else is behind you
  put out your hand – help them if you can.

The chain of life keeps clicking
  on and on throughout all time.
Say a prayer, close your eyes.
  you've made it, you will be fine.

TOBY 07/21/95

I had some quiet years after I had confronted my abuser. But very quickly I started to realize I was changing; well, my body was changing. I was starting to develop and there was hair under my arms and down below. I was glad at first that it was happening for me. After my first period there was a lull until the next one. It is obvious that soon I wished I were not maturing. With the coming of age also comes the worry of a child that someone may take over the shadow's place. There were a few years of worry as family members became the ones to stay away from. I cherish the good times, remember the teaching times, have scars from the hands of trusted people and came out of it without thinking of killing myself or anyone else. Through the years I have had conversations with other people that many families have similar events. As a child/woman it scared the heck out of me. As a parent I became overly alert. As a grandparent I watch closely to see if an intervention of sorts is needed.

As I became a teenager and attended high school, I formed bonds with a few other girls and a couple guys. I found hanging in a group was much better than hanging with just girls. I also, knew guy friends were easier to talk to. I had a couple guys that did not want to be a flirt, just hang. One would listen to anything I wanted to talk about. He would let down his veil once in awhile and we would just sit in silence after, watching the stars in the sky. After knowing him over a few years I would have jumped at the chance to date. I was too shy around him as a friend to tell him and he felt the same about me. We did talk about this about a week before I was to be married. Too late to act upon it. I, recently, noticed he is wooing a cousin of mine. I hope they find happiness. They both deserve that!

If I woke up tomorrow
    And found my world had changed,
I know there is one thing
    That would always stay the same.
There's nothing that could
    Take away the love I have for you
No matter what could happen
    My love for you would pull through.

If something came between us
    I'd still hand onto our love.
I'd move mountains for you.
    I'd ask help from God above.
No one could ever take away
    The feeling within my heart
You are always on my mind
    In my soul even when apart.

If throughout our busy lives
    I happen to forget my love for you
I'd stop myself – somehow
    And make sure you knew.
What it is that makes me whole

Is knowing how much you care for me.
Without my love for you
 I couldn't be whole; I just wouldn't be.

So when I fall asleep tonight
 I'll sleep a sleep content
Because no matter what may happen
 I've a love that was heaven sent.
Nothing could ever separate
 Me from this love I've inside.
And life is all worth living
 With you right by my side.

TOBY

In another world and another time, we might have stood a chance. That brings up the thought that we have parallel universes, and you meet people that are meant to be part of your life. And when you choose a different path then the other there is a different outcome. I wonder if I was as lonely there as here and possibly, he was lonely there also.

YOU MUSTN'T FEEL ALONE

You mustn't feel alone
    each night when you go asleep.
You are in my thoughts
    within my heart so deep
Life hasn't just passed you by
    even though it may feel that way.
There are many reasons to continue
    getting through each day.
Reach out to me
    I'll take your hand in mine.
I'm sure we can help
    each other – things will be fine.
Many times, I've wanted
    to tell you what it is I hide.
I've almost told you –
    let you see my other side.
Let's just suffice to say
    it's for you I deeply care.
So don't feel so down
    I have secrets with you to share.
I've built a shelter
    deep within my heart.
It's big enough for you
    if you want a little part.
I would protect you
    from all the sorrow and pain.
All you have to do
    is ask – I have no shame.

TOBY 06/11/95

I really prayed to God many times throughout my teenage life. It was always a simple prayer, and I did not write them all down. This is just one of many.

As I lay me down to sleep
I pray to God my sanity to keep
If I should lose it before I wake
Please grab a hold and give me a shake
If I should stay sane another day
Please say a prayer and show me the way.

TOBY 10/09/95

I wish I could go back to a simpler time and know that God would have shown me the way if only I had been receptive to His signs. I know if I had taken the signs, I would have saved a lot of misery within my short life, but also, I would have missed out on some of the most awesome people a person could meet. I know each one was in my life by chance. I would like to think that it was by design though. Whether a person came into my life and turned it upside down or simply created a loving memory I appreciate them all. A lot of learning in every relationship.

John and I tried to collaborate on a few of our songs. We wanted to do something together. I would say it was good because I liked what came of it. The frustration of collaborating with another human was not good. When John and I first got to know one another, we thought about being a duo. He was a fantastic guitarist and had great ideas for songs. I love the songs he has written. The main obstacle was we sing on the same level. I am an alto, and he is a high tenor, so our voice range sits on the same notes. I can harmonize with him if he records a song, but if we sing together, it all sounds the same. If I go up to harmonize, he goes with me. It was funny. It was not hilarious.

Alone I am not
>When I'm with you.
Afraid I am not
>To give my love to you.
>Why is it I laugh
>>When I want to cry?
>Why is all I feel
>>Hidden beyond my eyes?
Loved is how I am
>When in your dear arms
Knowing that you will
>Always keep me from harm.
>How do I tell you
>>The depth my loves goes?
>How do I show you
>>Just so you do know?
Touched is something
>I feel when I'm with you.
I can cry or laugh
>And you'd know just what to do.
>Do you know inside
>>Of me burns a deep desire?
>Do you think that you
>>Can handle all this fire?
I'll love you forever
>And I'll give all I've for you.
You saved me, my love
>Now I return that to you too.

KAL 05/03/96

John was truly a Godsend and I have given him my heart. We do not
have a perfect marriage, but who does. And more to the point I do
not know anyone that could honestly say their marriage was perfect.
The difference between a perfect marriage and my marriage is respect
that the other one has a difference of opinion and be willing to hear
it. We banter, we discuss, we get miffed, but we always love each
other.

I'm thinking of you, are you thinking of me?
All that we've done; more that can be
I'm dreaming of you, are you dreaming of me?
Fantasies galore now, things that could be

I'm loving you more; are you loving only me?
Passion is rising here; I need you to feel me
I'm wanting to be with you, are you wanting to be with me?
Being together is nearing; I'm waiting patiently.

I'm hoping for happiness; are you thinking of being happy?
A smile comes across my face when your smile I see
I'm running to you now; are you ready for me?
We hang onto each other, our future together I see.

KAL 17/09/20

When we were apart it was so hard. Although being apart made our love stronger I think, it also was hard on our souls. I wrote weekly to John along with my Mom and a few others in the family.

She truly loves him dear
Although they are so many miles apart
She worries how he is doing
And if he loves her with all his heart
They write many letters
Every day of every week.
Telling each other their days
While the tears seem to leak
Not knowing that both of them
Cling to their last and final kiss
Not wanting to tell each other
The pain of loss, the hugs they miss
The truth is they both despair
And long each of their days away
Hanging onto the phone
Crying warm tears each call, each day
When no one is looking
They both close their eyes and pray
That soon it will be all over;
That they be together again one day
The sun will shine brightly

On their faces when they meet again
Their eternal love will soar high
Tears of joy will fall like soft rain

KAL 17/09/09

Time should heal wounds more quickly, but some remain open way too long. I try to deal with my insecurities by myself. I know I should reach out and allow someone to guide me to being a healthy person. That is hard and I know my parents loved me throughout my life. I hold my memories of my childhood, well at least the happy ones, close to my heart. It is those unpleasant memories that hold my inner self hostage. Sometimes I can wash over them quite easily, but it is true that I still allow them to fester deep within my core. Writing about my life helps to heal some what, but I do know that I must talk to someone else before the healing can be complete. I thank God I had my parents, that He gave me the best parents and even though the devil being the shadow on the wall, they made life better for me.

There is love always nearby,
    Even though I've not yet seen.
I know whenever I would need it
    This love is there, and it's always been.

    There are two special people
        Even though I've not been round.
    Mean a lot to many people, including me.
        They are the best of folk ever to be found.

There is a place called heaven
    Even though I've not been there,
I can feel it all around me,
    In the eyes of people that care.

    There is a place I call home
        Even though I've not returned,
    I hold its memory deep,
        It's safe there I've learned.

There is always a time to find your way home
    Even though I've not yet done.

Now may be the time to head that way,
    But please take my hand and with me come.

TOBY 02/10/95

John healed a lot of wounds within my heart. He tells everyone that
he is a simple man and that means he does not think fast on his feet
or say the right thing, but he is honestly the best medicine I have. He
is the love I waited for. The only thing I wonder is why did God put
me through hell to find him. When I first met John, he was a long-
haul trucker. He tells me that he had thoughts of just driving his truck
over the edge and end his pain. He knew where and just had to get up
the nerve.

As I stare out of my window, I see a shooting star
My gaze watches as it goes from near to afar
I make a wish quietly a prayer only known to me
Hoping that it comes true, I will have to wait and see

As I walk through the forest, I find a four-leaf clover
I might have missed it if I hadn't just stepped over
I hold it close, say a loud prayer only known to me
Hoping that it comes true, I will have to wait and see

As I stroll down the lane there, I spot a shiny penny
That makes no sense knowing no one walks here but me
I pick it up, hold it tight and say a prayer only known to me
Hoping that it comes true, I will have to wait and see

As I go to turn down my light, I finally can see you
Three times I prayed for love and fate answered it true
I run into your open arms; my prayer was also known to you
No longer hoping, no waiting, just seeing it has all come true.

KAL 17/02/25

I know I have a small portion of PTSD created by my shadow
monster, but when I feel sorry for myself, I cannot help but
remember what my daughter went through. Her husband was more
than just someone she had loved; he was someone I trusted. I
remember on her wedding day, my husband, John, told him that he

may not be Kayla's father, but he would go to his grave to protect her and if he ever hurt her, he would be there to protect her in a heartbeat. Sadly, no one knew what was going on behind closed doors. I pray my daughter and her children can live their lives without fearing anyone. I am so proud of her because she finally stood up and got out with the kids. She had raised them so well. He on the other hand has lost all my trust and I pray that he looks to God for forgiveness and mends his future ways. I am not a person who condemns others easily. He deserves what he gets and any uncomfortable feelings or pain that comes into his life, I pray he realizes what she endured at those hands.

I TRUSTED YOU

Saw you as a child and knew the pain you'd seen.
Watched you grow up and knew the pain in which had been.

I knew all the bad, and yet, I trusted you.
I knew the life you'd had, and yet, I trusted you.

You promised to love her, to care for her & be there for her.
You promised to protect her, to never let harm bring pain to her.

I knew all the bad, and yet, I trusted you.
I knew the life you'd had, and yet, I trusted you.

You swore nobody would make my babies cry
You swore nobody would and now it's you that made them cry.

I knew all the bad, and yet, I trusted you.
I knew the life you'd had, and yet, I trusted you.

I trusted you to be a man, I trusted you to protect & stand.
I trusted, I trusted, I trusted you, no more are you a trusted man.

I knew all the bad, and yet, I trusted you.
I knew the life you'd had, and yet, I trusted you my lol.

I knew all the bad, and yet, I trusted you.
I knew the life you'd had, and yet, I trusted you.

KAL 17/11/14

Going back to my first husband and where I was when I finally made the decision to get out. I have never blamed him for our love diminishing. Why, because he was not equipped with the tools to be a strong husband. He did his best and I still have love for him as a father and person. And it is not his problem that deadened me inside over and over. Do not get me wrong, we loved each other and had quite a few years of love together and the most amazing children. With all this I still felt alone on my best days. I made myself busy with many outside groups and work. At least when I was busy, I could not hurt. This also was mainly the onset of my fibromyalgia. It is hard to smile when you are feeling desolate and alone. I would be happy and bam, there was the memory of what had happened as a child.

Though I'm very fond of you
And this will be hard to say
I can't be more than a friend
Because I need to find my own way

You make me smile and feel fine
I hope I do the same
We can still find time to be together
But love is not the name.

We can laugh and hug together
And make silly grins
We can love like friends
But more passion with us will never win.

I am not able to give my soul
And that's what you deserve
I can only offer my friendship
No more than that I haven't the nerve.

We spoke of feelings and that was good
You and I think alike
But I do belong deep in my heart
To someone else – I'd give him my life.

I've thought long and hard
And though it may feel wrong
I can't love you no matter what
My heart to another does belong.

You must always be secure
And know what a fine man you are
You deserve the best and more
You will in life go far.

KAL 03/15/96

When I was younger, I would start a poem or dedication and then sometimes years later would twist it into a song. This one was just the chorus to begin with and then I rewrote it twice to become two similar songs. Writing is a good release on my soul. Many times, I can just feel a little lighter after sitting down and composing. I, recently, played a couple of my songs for a friend and read as many of my poems. I hand picked the ones she would benefit hearing and felt good giving her a smile for the day. That is one of the reasons I do write. It is for others' benefits also.

How it affects me is personal, for sure. The benefit of seeing someone hear my creations and react positively is so healing. When someone reacts with tears, it also is good for me. I see that I am not the only one trying to grasp a healthier and happier life.

I love to give to other people, and I know my soul needs the contact with certain people in my life. I can feel how they are feeling even when they smile. I love that I can touch their heart just a little.

LORD IF YOU ARE LISTENING # 1

I cried the day you went away
I dried my tears and went on
Then I had nothing more to say
So, I was gone before long

You never reached out for me
And I was lost you know
I packed my bags yet again
I was gone before the first the first snow.

Lord, if you're listening
Please make me a blue bird
So, I can fly away home
Lord is you're listening
Please make me a blue bird
So, I can fly away home

I heard from someone today
Said that God had called you home
I thought about you again

And now I feel all alone

Lord, if you're listening
Please make me a blue bird
So, I can fly away home
Lord, if you're listening
Please make me a blue bird
So, I can fly away home

I wonder if I will ever smile
I miss where I use to be
I need to see my home
Lord, can you hear me

Lord, if you're listening
Please make me a blue bird
So, I can fly away home
Lord, if you're listening
Please make me a blue bird
So, I can fly away home

KAL 02/26/15

LORD IF YOU ARE LISTENING #2

I stand before you today
I get down on my knees
When I had nothing more to say
I was gone before long

You never completely left me
And I was lost you know
I packed my bags yet again
I was gone before the first the first snow.

Lord, if you're listening
Please make me a blue bird
So, I can fly away home
Lord is you're listening
Please make me a blue bird
So, I can fly away home

I heard from someone today

Said that I should come back home
I thought about you again
And how I feel all alone

Lord, if you're listening
Please make me a blue bird
So, I can fly away home
Lord, if you're listening
Please make me a blue bird
So, I can fly away home

I wonder if I will ever smile
I miss where I use to be
I need to see my home
Lord, can you hear me

Lord, if you're listening
Please make me a blue bird
So, I can fly away home
Lord, if you're listening
Please make me a blue bird
So, I can fly away home

KAL 03/02/16

Life loves to throw curve balls at us all. You can be on top of the world one moment and within seconds fall to the bottom of despair. Please know this happens to everyone. We are not unique in this aspect. More often than not we question what we are doing or what is next.

I am exactly as this next poem indicates. I know life will continue no matter what I must deal with and today may or may not be better than tomorrow. I know what has transpired in my life from the past and try diligently to not repeat errors and sadness. Although sometimes it just happens. I deal with it in my way and each time it may be different how I do. You may deal with situations that are exactly opposite of myself. That is perfectly okay. *You do you and I do me.* That is something I remind myself daily.

SPINNING LIKE A TOP

Spinning like a top, my life continues on.
I'm up, I'm down. I hear an endless sound.

Finding it so hard to balance myself today.
Yesterday was better; tomorrow come what may.

Spinning like a top, my life continues on.
I'm up, I'm down. I hear an endless sound.

Wanting to do more with my time at hand
Searching around me, where will I land?

Spinning like a top, my life continues on.
I'm up, I'm down. I hear an endless sound.

Seeing it all through, up to the very end.
Believing I'm okay until the angels are sent.

Spinning like a top, my life continues on.
I'm up, I'm down. I hear an endless sound.

KAL 17/09/23

I must admit that when I finish some poem or song, I will set it aside. Days, if not months, later I will review what I have wrote. Many times, I have to make sure it was mine. Many times, I see a note jotted down in poetic verse. I read it and think damn that is good. Then I realize it is my handwriting.

Talking of handwriting I have never been able to write the same way. My signature can be totally different with no similarities to previous ones. I have concluded that when I wrote or signed something, I am overcome by someone else's thoughts. Okay, maybe sometimes it is just Tobika. I feel so much pain in the world it is hard to cope in crowds. Whenever I shop, I just want to run in and get what I need and get out quickly. Christmas time is brutal on me. I get into a crowded space and wham I am feeling so many thoughts from the others around me. When I write next, I will search my soul for ideas. That is when I write like the following....

`Sometimes it`s the simplest form of life that can mean the most`.

I have down times in my day. I used to cover up the tough times with work or helping others. Lately though I sit down during these tough times and reflect. I find when this happens, I lose track of time. If I am in bed, I dream. I dream so much that it scares me awake. My mind takes me back to childhood and I change the course of what happened to see the outcome of my life. Most times it is not a welcomed outcome. Those nightmares help me see that life as it is may be the best outcome so far. A few make me think I should have gone down a different road. Cannot change the past though I can change how I choose today.

That is the unique fact of life – we can choose. If I had chose to stay in my first marriage it is possible, I wouldn't be alive today. I say that, but not in a bad way. What I mean is I was unhappy. I was losing myself within my own soul. I was so lost I was withdrawing from society. If I had chose to go north and meet up with Steve, I am confident that I would never made my way west and probably would have lost all contact with my children and family. Choices made form our lives.

When I grow up, I will be in control
When I grow up, I won't hurt anyone
Wait a second for me to think more
Wait a second for me not to run
I want to just go far away
I want to stay here without fear
Hold on now as I make sure
Hold on now as the coast clears

Will I ever feel safe and confident?
Will I ever trust others ever again?
Put away my dolls and toys under my bed
Put away my happiness and learn to defend
There are reasons I stay up late
There are reasons I don't want to sleep
Just one person takes away your life
Just one person can make you weep

As I turn away from the mirror
As I turn away from things I love
To compensate my inner insecurity
To compensate I don't gather, I shove
Will time fade away the memory?
Will time fade the terror, the pain?
I hang my head and try to forget
I hang my head and think of the shame

Do I wish ill on those who hurt me?
Do I wish I didn't carry this fright?
I'm trying hard each and every day
I'm trying hard not to fade from sight
I hope I have forgiven and carried on
I hope I have overcome my deepest pain
How do I make sense from all of this?

How do I make choices that don't wane?
I will try hard to look forward today
I will try hard to not think I'm at fault
The day may be longer than I like
The day may make me think of this assault
I put away all the thoughts for today
I put away all pain until tonight
This is the hardest part of each day
This is the way I stand up and fight

KAL 15/03/02

Every day I am trying to be better. When life is getting too much to manage my body shut itself off. I get a brain fog from the fibromyalgia. My aches and pains take control of my body. I do try not to let it win. I keep moving about and keep busy. But I do find reminiscing thoughts creeping into my brain. And some self-doubts also unfortunately. I play scenarios in my mind to make my brain shut off at night. Sometimes it works and sometimes it ends up scaring the life out of me. The shadow creeps in when that happens, and I feel trapped again. It is suffocating to say the least. It holds me captive again and I have to fight like hell to release myself. Over fifty years later and it still affects me.

May your tomorrows be
    brighter
Your hearts less
    laden.
Your faith grows
    stronger.
And your troubles start
    fading.

TOBY 03/02/95

When nothing is going right
And you start to feel blue,
Just say to yourself,
"I'm doing my best and that'll have to do!"

I think of all the young women I have met with challenges of drug addiction or prostitution. Their thoughts scream for help whether their words come out and ask. They all want a different life and would love to be without the addictions. I feel their pain within my soul and know most would rather die then say aloud they want out. They have no one to support their want to live life; there are too many pushing them to continue as they are. It is so sad. They have dreams, but no security to live clean. And while they were incarcerated there was no real aids or courses that made sense to help them. They needed tough love and concerned therapists. They should have had courses to help wean off from whichever drug they had been on. Keeping them 'high' through the medicinal method does not work. Yes, there were chores to do, but menial chores that did not require being proud of accomplishment. The longer they stay the dumbing down shows. I know as it affected me. You do not show your 'normality' or 'educational prowess.' You cannot help but become as they are because there are more of them than you and they do not understand being part of community.

Going back to reality and life without bars. That was hard. The adjustments I had to make before my stay lingered and I had to try and become normal. I stayed in an apartment for two weeks before being allowed home. While there I was overcome with writing, and I have a feeling it was not from the girls below me. I am sure the supervisor in the office behind my place was going through a lot. I got a chance to talk to her a little as I would leave my door open in the kitchen, so it felt like I was there with someone. She was a wonderful and kind lady.

Whenever I write like this my memories flood back and I will be honest with everyone; these memories are not welcomed in my life. The little girl points out that my life could have been much better. At least, my life had not ended as other people that have gotten on the wrong track. My shadow seems so much smaller than most women I have sat and spoke with about their upbringing. Theirs had sexual attacks that stayed with them their whole life. Most were familiar people; their father, their mother's lover, their brother, their uncle, their best friend's dad, and a few had female attackers. Man, I felt their pain and tried to sum it up into something understandable. These women deserve more than a second chance, they deserve all the happiness in the world. They lived a much more damaging life and yet there we were, sharing accommodations. The irony of life. The road may be different and difficult, but the end could be the same.

"Light and shadow are opposite sides of the same coin. We can illuminate our paths or darken our way. It is a matter of choice."
— Maya Angelou

When I started writing this, I didn't think I would be able to say what I needed to. I thought that I would not have enough to say. I knew it would be muddled and jump around. I wanted to let people know that we all have hang ups, we all have memories, we have trauma, we get lost, we feel inadequate, and we feel alone at times. That said, we also have love to give and love to receive. There are lots of ways to move on. There are people who can help. We can grow from anything. We are not alone, and we don't have to feel lonely. Friends come in all forms. Love comes from unexpected people.

A smile is just a smile
Unless it's given to you.

A hug is just a hug
Until it's only for you.

A tear is just a tear
Unless it's shed for you.

A friend is just a friend
Until they are there for you.

TOBY 05/14/95

I have had many friends come into my life and most have gone on to other adventures. It is the friends that stood up for me that made me stronger. They were my heroes also. I could never name all of them, but I want them to know I love them all. Thank you to Lori, Sherry, Kathy, Bev, Lavie, Carl, Bob S, Trish, Bre, Bob M, Connie, Sherri, Gwenda, Jeff, John D, - to name a few from past to present.

I have a dream where I was not attacked at any time. I go through life sailing without any drama. You know what it was a boring dream. The great part was not having that shadow on the wall. The sad part is most of my loved ones are not there. My children are not born. My first marriage is my only marriage although it is not with my first husband. The good part is John is still my husband. His first marriage did not happen either. The first time I had this dream I woke up and wrote how I say my dream felt to me. I wish I could shout to the world how special this man is. I lucked out that he dropped everything for me, and I thank God that I chose him too.

Stay if only for a minute
    Don't leave until you see
Stay if only for a minute
    You never know what will be
Stay if only for a minute
    The world can wait for you
Stay if only for a minute
    There's something we must do
Stay if only for a minute
    Sixty seconds to change our life
Stay if only for a minute
    The extra time would be nice
Stay if only for a minute
    There has to be time for us
Stay if only for a minute
    One minute alone could be enough.
Stay if only for a minute
    Then together our hearts to meet.
Stay if only for a minute
    Our love final and now complete

STAY!!!

KAL 17/09/23

I can only imagine that those of us with scars from the past, move on and get clear. No amount of dreaming has erased what happened. The shadow on the wall diminishes over time, but I remember. The pain has almost disappeared, yet it can come back when you least expect it.

The more you talk about your trauma, the better you can feel. A professional therapist may make more sense of how a person relates to it, but it still is there. All I can say is that I feel better writing about it. I can see the light beaming into my childhood bedroom and it banishes the shadow back into oblivion.

Do what is necessary to heal. Forgiveness works only if you forgive yourself also. Take all the time you need to better your life. Work away from your trauma. If you can, see someone that can help you. If you cannot, talk to anyone, whether it is a trusted loved one or a complete stranger that just listens.

I am so grateful that I did not turn to drinking or drugs to push away what had happened. I was lucky. I know that I was always one step away from going down that path. It would have been easy with my first husband's family life. I am sorry that I fell and ended up at Camp Cupcake. I still remain lucky in my mind. My loving husband, friends and family made adjustments for me, and I cannot ever repay the love and support. They probably will never realize how much they mean to me. They are a big part of helping chase away the shadow.

No matter how long it takes you to figure out life or your past, keep plodding along. Frustration is going to be a key factor in weighing you down. Do not give up. Do not give in. Take breaks when you need one, just make sure you save your work and make sure you are willing to lay it all out for yourself to heal.

FRUSTRATION

It seems so impossible,
I don't understand.
I think I've got it,
Now it's out of hand.
I think I'm done,
But can't you see.
I write it down,
I read it over,
I rub it out.
Then I start over.
I'm just so FRUSTRATED
I don't know what to do.
It's making me blue.
I put it together,
It falls apart.
All this FRUSTRATION
Is breaking my heart.

I'M SO FRUSTRATED!!

Toby with help of Jaymee

My husband wrote this song and my sister, Colleen, and I sang
harmony for him. I mentioned we sang a song together and this was
one that made me fall in love even more with him. He wrote it
completely and we took the chance to sing with John. Each time we
three were together, at some point, this song would be sung together.

That first kiss it was something.
It was like they're both starving
For the passion that neither of them knew
Now they're both kinda the same,
Trying to soothe their pain
In the sweet loving arms of someone new.

Now, some say it ain't right
But that's the way it is.
They're gonna love tonight.
Cause it's something they both miss.

And where's it all going, they got no way of knowing.
For a little while they can both **try to forget**
For a little while they can both **try to forget.**

Now they've been living lonely
They both know it's only
For the lack of the kind of loving they both need.
And sometimes late at night
They lay in the dark and cry
For the hunger they just can't seem to forget.

Now, some say it ain't right
But that's the way it is.
They're gonna love tonight.
Cause it's something they both miss.
And where's it all going, they got no way of knowing.
For a little while they can both **try to forget**
For a little while they can both **try to forget.**

JOHN BUB BURGESS 1996

I am willing to admit now that I should have spoken up and let the adults take charge years ago. It would have changed my path, I am sure. It may have also not given me a creative edge, but we will never know. Life is funny and our fates are written before we get to the end. Thank you, God, for seeing me through. I am grateful for my life, my family, my plight. Does not mean I am any less confused.

How about you? Confused? Join the club. Better yet, you do you, no matter the consequences, live your best life!! Be brave, be you! Do not let your shadows win over your life. Do not think you are not worth dealing with the trauma and breaking free of your chains! You are worth it, and your story is important.

I sat back and reread everything I have written and more came pouring out. Every day brings more feelings and thoughts. Some days I cannot hear for the silence and other days I can't think for the void inside. I love the days I hear that little voice saying I can do this. I love the days that I feel so good inside that nothing could take the smile off my face. I pray for more of those days in the future. I believe I have managed to shed a lot of my fears.

What I will say to anyone is this....

I will smile more and yet I will still wonder if I am where I should be. I will go forward and take precautions to not let anything ruin my day. I shall reach out to anyone that I can help, and I will allow others to help me more.

Just as a final note to myself. I know I will have days that nothing makes sense that is okay as I will adapt. It takes a lot of courage to be happy. I do not accept that I do not matter anymore. I will conquer those feelings. I will live each day with the fulfilment of love and acceptance. I know who I am.

In my mind I can clearly see
What it is I want to be

I'm not this person that you see
But someone so different from me

I am confident and sure of what I do
So happy and strong looking at life anew

No more shadows fall across my eyes
And all the truths outweigh the lies

I have a smile that is so very bright
So easy going and doing what is right

I no longer feel that I'm out of touch
But instead enjoying life so much

It doesn't matter what others may think
Comforting to myself and insecurities did shrink

I'm proud of who I have now become
Out of the darkness and into the sun

Trouble no longer makes me feel ill
Because I am mighty and now strong willed

If others could see this form of me

They'd know I'm able to help them also be free.

I am so fortunate to be alive today
But I will be this person that only I see

I have to control how others make me feel
All their pain makes it hard to deal

The powers within me are getting so strong
To live as my other is what I do long

KAL. 21/03/03

I found this in my phone today with a few other poems. I really do not remember writing it, but Toby still has a voice and wants to let out some more. Who am I to keep her bound inside? I guess we will all see what she has in store for me and for everyone around her.

LIFE IS WONDERFUL

Life is wonderful
(Even though I feel worthless)
I love waking each day
(Worrying if I'm good enough)

I can only smile
(Because no one understands)
When others look my way
(I know they think I'm rough)

The day brings laughter
(But inside I shed tears)
I think I'll go for a walk
(That would be useless)
I want to express my love
(Will it be accepted)
I stand in a crowd
(Although I'm alone)

I feel what others think
(And it's killing me inside)
I see the pain others feel
(It hurts me within my soul)
I want to show happiness
(It's hard when you are crying)
I need to change myself
(Will it ever be enough)

I hear what others say
(I have done nothing wrong)
I try and maintain my emotions
(It's hard knowing their hatred)
Others don't realize I see them
(And yet I continue to smile)
They think I don't know
(Can I go on in life?)

KAL 21/09/25

Be you, find what you can do to release your troubles, the secret to my healing is mostly….me. I will do what I must. But I will not resort to drugs, alcohol, or suicide to heal. That only brings trouble to those who love you. That will never heal a person. Please reach out to someone that can help you if you have trauma or troubles that need healing. Your voice is important to more than just you. Your shadows can be conquered, and the first step is telling yourself it is okay to know the shadow lingers. Don't let the shadows win!!!

And the shadow slowly fades…….

I want to tell you to love yourself. Find your muse. See your talent. Reach out and change what needs to be fixed. Mine was poetry, lyrics, and family Yours can be anything you imagine. Do not ever let the shadows in your life control the best 'YOU'. I fought a long time to find myself. And when I look back, I appreciate the person I had to be to protect myself (and Toby). Today Toby is still on board, and she can allow me to have memories and see my own strength.

Life is hard, live regardless!!
Have a great day and see you at the top!

ABOUT THE AUTHOR –

Kim Burgess took the pen name of TOBY in 1974 and changed it to KAL in 1996. Under these pen names she has created many poems, musical compositions, and verses. Kim is the youngest of seven children and raised in Southwestern Ontario. As she has always said, she was one of the second Corinthians living in the garden of Eden which is just down the road from the land of Goshen. She will also tell you she had to leave Eden to find Heaven which is Cranbrook BC.

Family members, events and just inspirations were her start in writing. She also admired her paternal grandpa, Leslie Winfred Pressey, as he would sit at his table and hum his own songs over and over with verses he had written. Kim feels that if at least one person is made to feel a little lighter and happier, then she has achieved her purpose.

To Tree – Thanks for your input and insights. To Sherry – Thanks buddy you were the best. To John – I thank God every day for you in my life. To my children and grandchildren – I am because you are.

We all have bumps in the road, but with the love and support of family and friends we can overcome all hardships. Thank you for being my people and my circus!

May your future be bright, alive, and successful.

Kim Burgess//KAL/TOBY

www.ingramcontent.com/pod-product-compliance
Lightning Source LLC
Chambersburg PA
CBHW051150120626
46547CB00012B/1020